Wittgenstein's Philosophy of Psychology

International Library of Philosophy

Editor: Ted Honderich
Grote Professor of the Philosophy of Mind and Logic
University College London

Wittgenstein's Philosophy of Psychology

Malcolm Budd

Routledge
London and New York

First published 1989
by Routledge
11 New Fetter Lane, London EC4P 4EE
29 West 35th Street, New York, NY 10001

Disc conversion by Columns, Typesetters of Reading
Printed in Great Britain by
T.J. Press (Padstow) Ltd. Padstow, Cornwall.

British Library Cataloguing in Publication Data

Budd, Malcolm, 1941–
  Wittgenstein's philosophy of psychology.
  (International library of philosophy).
  1. Psychology. Theories of Wittgenstein,
  Ludwig, 1889–1951
  I. Title II. Series
  150'.92'4

ISBN 0–415–03439–6

Library of Congress Cataloguing in Publication Data

Budd, Malcolm, 1941–
  Wittgenstein's philosophy of psychology/Malcolm Budd.
  p. cm. — (International library of philosophy)
  Bibliography: p.
  Includes index.
  1. Psychology—Philosophy. 2. Wittgenstein,
    Ludwig, 1889–1951–
  Contributions in psychology. I. Title. II. Series.
  BF38.B84 1989
  150'. 1—dc19   88–23981 CIP

'How can one learn the truth by thinking?
As one learns to see a face better if one draws it.'

Ludwig Wittgenstein
Zettel 255

CONTENTS

vii

Contents

Contents

PREFACE

The three areas to which Wittgenstein devoted his greatest
energies in the second half of his life were the philosophy of
language, the philosophy of mathematics and the philosophy of
psychology. His thoughts in these different fields intersect in
numerous ways and it is not possible to examine adequately his
contribution to one of these subjects in total isolation from his
treatment of related issues in the others. This is especially true of
his philosophy of psychology, for not only is it imbued with his
later thoughts about the nature and understanding of language,
but a considerable part of his interest in the philosophy of
psychology derived from his dissatisfaction with his early
philosophy of language and its underlying conception of mental
representation. What I have tried to do is to disentangle the main
threads of Wittgenstein's philosophy of psychology from his more
general philosophy of language, but only in so far as the resulting
picture remains a faithful image of his thought. Although the
lines I have traced overlap with ones that extend into other areas
of philosophy and elaborations of the picture I have drawn are
possible at many points, I believe that only a misplaced piety
would baulk at the attempt.

Wittgenstein's work in the philosophy of psychology can be
considered from two points of view: its relevance to psychology
and its importance within philosophy. Wittgenstein claimed that
the science of psychology is barren and confusion is endemic in it.
This is not due, he maintained, to the fact that psychology is a
young science that is still struggling to find appropriate ways to

investigate its subject matter. The kind of confusion that reigns in psychology is, he believed, conceptual confusion: psychologists are prone to unclarity about everyday psychological concepts and the sophisticated experimental methods they employ fail to deal satisfactorily with the problems addressed, which are really of a philosophical nature. These problems can be resolved, so Wittgenstein thought, only by gaining a proper understanding of the psychological concepts from which they arise. His own work in the philosophy of psychology attempts to represent our ordinary psychological concepts in such a manner that the problems that stem from confusion about the nature of these concepts are dissolved. And it is here that its interest to philosophy lies, whether or not its claims about the science of psychology are unfounded, exaggerated, or dated.

I have not attempted to provide a comprehensive treatment of Wittgenstein's work in the philosophy of psychology: it is hard to understand what this would be. Moreover, even if it were possible to give a truly comprehensive account, I am sure this would not be desirable. It may be true that the treatment of each psychological concept casts light on the correct treatment of all. That was Wittgenstein's claim. But the extraordinarily large number and great variety of psychological concepts that Wittgenstein examines (cursorily or at length), the numerous interconnections between his different psychological investigations, the provisional or uncertain nature of many of his remarks, and the recurrent themes and targets demand a selective treatment. It is certainly not true that Wittgenstein's treatment of each new psychological concept further illuminates his own philosophy of psychology.

It will be obvious to readers familiar with Wittgenstein's work that there are aspects of his thought about which I am silent: there are matters Wittgenstein thought about in an interesting way that I have not included and the subjects I have chosen to consider involve nuances and ramify in ways I have ignored. I have selected topics that highlight the distinctive features of Wittgenstein's approach to the philosophy of psychology and these topics include, I believe, his central contributions to the subject. What is needed for each of the topics is a vantage-point from which Wittgenstein's investigation can be most easily surveyed: I have tried to identify such a position and to use it to provide a perspicuous representation of his thought.

Wittgenstein's conception of the nature of philosophy is liable to render his examination of psychological concepts problematic for those with a different and more liberal conception of philosophy. For Wittgenstein is often concerned not so much to delineate the grammar of psychological words as to expose his reader to and inoculate him against seductive misconceptions of that grammar. Despite the hazardous nature of the enterprise, I have been particularly concerned to articulate what seem to be Wittgenstein's positive suggestions wherever there are traces of them, even if these traces are faint.

The references to Wittgenstein's writings in the Notes not only identify quotations, and places where Wittgenstein maintains (so I believe) the views I attribute to him, but also direct the interested reader to passages in Wittgenstein's works which develop the points in the text at greater length or which contain related considerations. It should not be forgotten that Wittgenstein published none of the works that contain his later philosophy and that have appeared since his death under his name. He would certainly have rejected many of the published remarks as inadequate, misleading, or mistaken.

Chapters II, III and IV are based upon three of my published papers: 'Wittgenstein on Meaning, Interpretation and Rules', *Synthese*, vol. 58 no. 3, March 1984, 'Wittgenstein on Sensuous Experiences', *The Philosophical Quarterly*, vol. 36 no. 143, April 1986, and 'Wittgenstein on Seeing Aspects', *Mind*, vol. XCVI no. 381, January 1987. These papers have all been rewritten, in places heavily, and there are both additions and omissions. I am grateful to Kluwer Academic Publishers and Basil Blackwell for permission to make use of this material. I am also grateful to Basil Blackwell for permission to quote from Wittgenstein's works.

My greatest debt is undoubtedly to Colin McGinn, with whom I frequently discussed Wittgenstein's work and also many issues in the philosophy of psychology when we were colleagues. His energy, clarity of mind, and cheerfulness have always had a beneficial effect on my own thinking. My discussions with him and the graduate seminar we gave on some aspects of

Wittgenstein's work were the stimulus that led to my decision to write this book. But he has not seen what I have written and is unlikely to agree with all of it.

I am grateful to Wendy Robins for the hard work she put into the preparation of the final typescript.

Malcolm Budd
1 June 1988

I

INTRODUCTION

WITTGENSTEIN'S CONCEPTION OF THE PHILOSOPHY OF PSYCHOLOGY

What did Wittgenstein understand by the philosophy of psychology? A skeleton answer would be this: the aim of the philosophy of psychology is the construction of perspicuous representations of everyday psychological concepts; this aim is achieved by the delineation of the grammar of psychological words; the importance of the philosophy of psychology derives from its underlying purpose, which is the dissolution of philosophical problems about the nature of the mind; these problems can be treated successfully only by attaining a synoptic view of the ordinary language of psychology; the philosophy of psychology is purely descriptive and in no way explanatory. But this answer must be fleshed out if it is to be illuminating.

We must begin from Wittgenstein's conception of the nature of philosophy. For he had a distinctive vision of philosophy that determined both the way he worked in any area of philosophy and what he tried to achieve. The foundation of his thought is that philosophical investigations are conceptual investigations.[1] Accordingly, his researches in the philosophy of psychology are researches into psychological concepts. But since there are very different kinds of investigation into concepts, the characterisation of Wittgenstein's philosophy of psychology as an investigation of psychological concepts is informative only in the light of a clear understanding of the kind of conceptual investigation he engaged in. Now Wittgenstein insisted that it would be misleading to describe such an investigation as a search for an *analysis* of a concept, if this suggests that there is something hidden in the concept that he wished to bring to light and that the discovery of this would be a new piece of information. On the contrary, he believed that everything of philosophical interest lies open to view and he regarded all the relevant facts about the concept as being already known. So there is nothing for which an *explanation* is being sought.[2]

But if this is so, what sort of enterprise is a conceptual investigation of the kind Wittgenstein practised? An initial answer is that it is an attempt to *describe the use of words* in which the concept under examination is manifested. It is therefore an investigation of what Wittgenstein referred to as the 'grammar' of words:

> Grammar describes the use of words in the language.[3]

> Grammar does not tell us how language must be constructed in order to fulfil its purpose, in order to have such-and-such an effect on human beings. It only describes and in no way explains the use of signs.[4]

The importance of the idea of grammar in Wittgenstein's thought is clearly revealed when seen against the background of the attitude to language that he adopted in his philosophical work. To put the matter briefly: he rejected the idea that the meanings of words should be explained by reference to psychological causes and effects of the use of words; he renounced any interest in an explanation of the operation of language as a psycho-physical mechanism;[5] he recommended his conception of the meaning of a word as its use in the language; and he restricted his philosophical examination of language to a description of its grammar.

It follows from this account of a conceptual investigation that Wittgenstein's philosophy of psychology is an investigation of psychological concepts (everyday psychological concepts)[6] restricted to the description of the use of psychological words. Now the construction and assessment of mind-models – hypothetical mental mechanisms postulated to explain psychological capacities, conscious experience and observed behaviour – is the task of the science of psychology, not philosophy. Hence, the nature of the mind and its activities, in the sense in which Wittgenstein was interested in them, is not concealed but lies open to view as it is revealed in the ways in which psychological words are used.[7]

But if Wittgenstein's aim was only to describe the use of psychological terms, what kind or kinds of description was he striving for? And why is a description of the required kind worth having? What is the importance of the investigation?

A preliminary answer to the first question is this: the kind of description of the use of psychological words that was the goal of Wittgenstein's investigation is not one that aims for exactness, but rather one that tries to achieve a synoptic view (a comprehensive view, a view of the whole) by means of a perspicuous representation (übersichtliche Darstellung):

> The concept of a perspicuous representation is of fundamental significance for us. It earmarks the form of account we give, the way we look at things.[8]

What is a perspicuous representation of the use of words? One of the few examples described by Wittgenstein *as* a perspicuous representation is the colour octahedron, which can be used as an illustration of the relations between colour-words and as showing what does and what does not make sense in the language of colour.[9] A perspicuous representation is not, however, a single kind of construction, but any way in which the use of words and the similarities and differences between uses of words in the language is clearly revealed. For there is no single way in which the kind of reflective understanding of the meanings of words Wittgenstein tried to make accessible can be achieved. He therefore needed to devise a number of methods for the creation of a perspicuous representation of the uses of words. Undoubtedly his most distinctive method was the invention of primitive forms of language, language-games, in which the ways in which words function are easy to grasp, and which throw light on our own language when used as objects of comparison, showing up both similarities and differences.[10]

We have seen that Wittgenstein wanted to achieve a certain kind of understanding of psychological concepts. This understanding is produced by a perspicuous representation of the use of psychological words and it consists in seeing the connections between them. It enables one to move easily from one to another: the ideal is a mastery of their similarities and differences akin to the mastery of a musician who can modulate from any key to any other.[11] And it is because Wittgenstein aimed to gain a synoptic view of psychological concepts that he explored so many of them: the treatment of each, he thought, casts light on the correct treatment of all.[12] But we have still not explained why a perspicuous representation and a synoptic view is a desirable goal.

Now it is an essential thesis of Wittgenstein's later philosophy that it is not easy for someone to describe correctly the way in which *he himself* uses a word; when he tries to do this he is liable to go wrong; and if he goes wrong in his description of a psychological word, he is enmeshed in a philosophical confusion about the mind.[13] The importance for Wittgenstein of the idea of a perspicuous representation of the grammar of words derives from the fact that philosophical confusions engendered by misunderstanding one's own language in reflection upon it are removed or discouraged by correct description of this synoptic kind. The kind of description he aspired to – an arrangement of what we have always known[14] – gains its significance from the philosophical problems in which one becomes entangled unless one has secured a bird's-eye view of the linguistic domain. Without such a viewpoint, the function of a psychological concept in our thought about the mind will be misrepresented or rendered problematic.

But why should it be hard to describe the use of a word correctly, if there is no difficulty in using it in the right way? Why doesn't our understanding of the word, our practical mastery of it, ensure that we do not fall into error if we set out to describe its use?

Wittgenstein offered many reasons against such a simple view of the matter. In the first place, there is the general point that the mastery of a technique and the ability to give an accurate account of the technique are very different capacities, and there is usually no good reason why someone who has acquired mastery of a technique should also be prepared to give an account of the technique he has mastered. In particular, a description of the grammar of a word is of no use in everyday life; only rarely do we pick up the use of a word by having its use described to us;

4

and although we are trained or encouraged to master the use of words, we are not taught to describe it. So it is quite possible that there should be a disparity between our technique of using a word and the description of this technique that we come up with when we reflect upon it. Wittgenstein produced numerous illustrations of how the possession of one ability does not guarantee the possession of a related, higher-level ability. One takes the form of imagining that we know our way around a city extremely well, in the sense that we find it easy to take the shortest route from any place in it to any other, but that we are unable to draw a map of the city: when we try we go completely wrong.[15] Another likens the relation between the ability to describe correctly the use of a word we have mastered and the mastery we possess to the relation between the ability to paint an accurate representation of someone and the ability to see the person clearly:

> When we want to describe the use of a word, – isn't it like
> wanting to make a portrait of a face? I see it clearly; the
> expression of these features is *well* known to me; and if I had
> to paint it I shouldn't know where to begin. And if I do
> actually make a picture, it is wholly inadequate. – If I had a
> description in front of me I'd recognize it, perhaps detect
> mistakes in it. But my being able to do that does not mean that
> I could myself have given the description.[16]

But this first point is only suggestive and it is compatible with our finding little difficulty in describing the ways in which we use words if we set our minds to it. Wittgenstein placed great emphasis on a different point: when we attempt to describe the use of words we are subject to pressures that distort the descriptions we give, usually in the direction of making our accounts over-simplified. For example, he believed that we are tempted to model our accounts on certain paradigms, as when we construe any adjective as designating an ingredient of whatever it applies to, or hypostatise an object to correspond to a name. The second of these temptations is one of the leading motives of his later philosophy, and plays a prominent role in Chapter III.

He also identified special problems that arise in giving an account of the grammar of *psychological* words. Two of these deserve attention. The first is that for many psychological words it is difficult to renounce all theory and to engage in mere description of the use of the words: we are tempted to explain, instead of restricting ourselves to description. And the reason why we experience this inclination is that the description appears to be obviously incomplete, so that we need to fill out the facts in order to understand them:

> It is as if one saw a screen with scattered colour-patches, and said: the way they are here, they are unintelligible; they only make sense when one completes them into a shape. – Whereas I want to say: Here *is* the whole. (If you complete it, you falsify it.)[17]

The second difficulty in giving a correct description of the use of a psychological word arises from the fact that the use of such a word is often tangled, unclear, ragged, widely ramified, fluid,[18] so that the situation we are faced with is like the one we would encounter if 'the word "violin" referred not only to the instrument, but sometimes to the violinist, the violin part, the sound, or even the playing of the violin'.[19] Wittgenstein claimed that it is only to be expected that psychological words should have tangled uses, for they are all everyday words and are therefore unlikely to have unified employments. And since the way in which any one of them is used is widely ramified, it is not easy to obtain a synoptic view of their use.[20] Moreover, the difficulty is aggravated, Wittgenstein believed, by the fact that it is natural for us to want to give a simple description of the use of a word. So we impose upon it an inappropriate pattern; but the use is more complex than the pattern to which we attempt to fit it, and the result is that exceptions to the rules we find ourselves insisting upon constantly arise.[21]

Now the fact that the use of the words 'believe', 'expect', 'fear', 'hope', 'intend', 'think' is variegated[22] means that it is possible to distinguish within the employment of a single psychological verb different kinds of use. It would therefore be possible for there to be a language in which these different kinds of use are marked by the employment of different words, so that where in our language a single word is used in a number of ways, in this other language a number of words are used, each with a unitary employment.[23] If this were so, then:

Perhaps the concepts of such a language would be more
suitable for understanding psychology than the concepts of our
language.[24]

But Wittgenstein showed no interest in the construction of a
language of this kind. The reason for this was not that he held a
special brief for the concepts of our own language. We have just
seen that he did not regard our own psychological concepts as
being specially suitable for understanding psychology, and a
language in which people as it were thought more definitely[25]
than we do would make the task easier. Moreover, he believed
that it is important not to assume that the concepts of our own
language are the uniquely *right* ones for intelligent human beings
to use. On the contrary, he argued that if we imagine certain
general facts of nature to be different from what they are, then
concepts different from our own will appear *natural* to us.[26]
Nevertheless, his own investigations in philosophy were directed
towards the concepts we actually operate with. And the reason
for this should now be clear: he was interested in language only
in so far as it is the source of philosophical difficulties.
Philosophical problems about the nature of the mind arise,
Wittgenstein believed, from confusion about the use of our own
psychological vocabulary, and this confusion can be dissipated
only by gaining a synoptic view of our own language of
psychology.

INTROSPECTION AND DEFINITION

But it might be thought that there is a better approach than the
one Wittgenstein advocates. For why should we attempt to
achieve a synoptic view of psychological concepts by such a
roundabout route – through a network of descriptions of the ways
in which words are used – when there is a more direct path open
to us, one easy to follow and certain to lead to our goal? No
reason has been given for denying ourselves access to introspection and thereby making the task more difficult than it need be.
For, so this line of thought continues, if we use the resources of
introspection, we can construct *definitions* of the various
psychological concepts, and these definitions will provide us at

once with the desired perspicuous representations. All we need to do is to wait for a certain psychological concept to apply to us (or to bring this about if it lies within our power to do so), and then attend to what goes on within our mind on that occasion: what we are aware of will be an instance of the concept and by describing what happens when the concept applies we express a definition of the concept. Since this definition will be in itself a perspicuous representation of the concept, and introspection can be used to construct a definition for any psychological concept, if our view of any concept is distorted it can be corrected by recourse to introspection.

There is much that is wrong with this suggestion. In the first place, the emphasis on definitions as perspicuous representations of grammar is misplaced. Although a definition can clarify the grammar of a word, even when a definition is available it may not provide the kind of insight into the role of a word in the language that Wittgenstein intended a perspicuous representation to produce.[27] Moreover, the search for a definition pins the investigation to a question of the unhelpful 'What is . . . ?' form.[28]

A more fundamental defect in the suggestion derives from the fact that *introspection can never lead to a definition*, but only to a psychological statement about the subject.[29] My use of introspection can show me only what is true for me, and only what is true for me on the occasion I introspect.[30] For no matter how careful I may be, *whatever* I am aware of happening when I introspect, the question must arise whether it is essential that this happening should occur in someone when the psychological predicate I am proposing to define applies to him. And I am faced with the following dilemma: either I already know before I introspect that it is essential, or I do not know that it is essential. But if I know in advance that it is essential, introspection is redundant. If, on the other hand, I do not already know that it is essential, introspection can be no help to me: I cannot be aware through introspection *that* this happening constitutes the essence of the psychological state signified by the predicate. Consider a simple example: I report that when I decided to visit my mother I was aware of a visual image of her. Now this is clearly of no use in constructing a definition of what it is to form an intention: it may have been true of me, but it does not need to be true of someone who forms a similar intention (myself on another occasion, for example). Since it is not of the essence of forming an intention that the subject should visualise some part of the content of the intention, what my introspection shows me does not put me into a position to define, even partly, the concept of forming an intention. I know this fact about the essence by reflection upon the concept of intention, and if I did not know it I would not be able to acquire the knowledge through introspection.

There is another reason for the inadequacy of introspection as a source of definitions of psychological concepts, which applies to many, but not all, psychological concepts. Whereas the first reason focuses on the impossibility that introspection should show one *that* a particular happening constitutes the essence of what a psychological predicate stands for, the second concerns the impossibility of being aware *of* the essence by means of introspection. For the use of introspection to define a psychological concept presupposes that the predicate signifies the intrinsic nature of what happens in a person's consciousness at the time when the predicate becomes true of him. If the application of the predicate is not determined by what is present to a person's consciousness at the time, it is not possible to be aware by means of introspection of anything that would suffice for a definition of the predicate. But there are many psychological predicates that do not designate a state of consciousness at all, or for which the intrinsic nature of what is before the mind is insufficient for the predicate to apply (as when the relation between the state of consciousness and something external to the state is relevant to whether the predicate applies).

Apart from these inadequacies, introspection would even so not be able to provide a synoptic view of psychological concepts by means of definitions. For the use of introspection could not be a *comprehensive* method for arriving at a perspicuous representation of the psychological realm. If we were to pursue this method, the words we would use to formulate any definition would be words that designate what happens in our consciousness. But these words would themselves be psychological words, standing as much in need of definition as any psychological predicate they are used to define. And it would be foolish to suppose that by the use of introspection we would be able to formulate a definition of a word that *does* stand for a content of consciousness. For the most that introspection could reveal would be the content of consciousness that the word designates, and we know in advance what the correct word for that state of consciousness is, namely, the word we are looking to define. Consider the predicate 'is in pain': what else should I expect to find in my consciousness when the predicate is true of me other than pain, and what other concept should I expect to bring it under than the concept of pain? Introspection therefore provides no view of the concept at all, and so no synoptic view. Hence:

> It shews a fundamental misunderstanding, if I am inclined to study the headache I have now in order to get clear about the philosophical problem of sensation.[31]

THE CLASSIFICATION OF PSYCHOLOGICAL CONCEPTS

Wittgenstein's published writings contain two schemes of classification of psychological concepts.[32] Each scheme belies its overall appearance: neither looks much like a description of the uses of psychological words, although each is intended to furnish such a description. In fact, the psychological categories distinguished in these classifications are determined by what are meant to be logical criteria[33] for inclusion in the category, and Wittgenstein's remarks are intended to be construed as grammatical, expressing the linguistic essence[34] of psychological kinds by reference to what it does and does not make sense to say of an instance of a kind. So the schemes are attempts to construct lucid representations of the grammar of psychological words. Neither scheme makes any claim to completeness (what would this be?), and there are numerous obvious omissions. The first classification is somewhat uncertain and highly schematic; the second, which is described as a plan for the treatment of psychological concepts, is considerably more accomplished and elaborate, although it is restricted to the concepts of sensations, images, and emotions. It would be wrong to consider either scheme as definitive of what it deals with, but each is characteristic of Wittgenstein's method of treatment of psychological concepts, and the second brings together many points he develops elsewhere and provides miniature studies of the concepts it depicts. The sketch of the concept of sensation is representative of the more accomplished scheme:

Sensations: their inner connexions and analogies.

All have genuine duration. Possibility of giving the beginning and the end. Possibility of their being synchronized, of simultaneous occurrence.

All have degrees and qualitative mixtures. Degree: scarcely perceptible – unendurable.

In this sense there is not a sensation of position or movement.

Place of feeling in the body: differentiates seeing and hearing from sense of pressure, temperature, taste and pain.

(If sensations are characteristic of the position and movements of the limbs, at any rate their place is not the joint.)

One *knows* the position of one's limbs and their movements. One can give them if asked, for example.

Just as one also knows the place of a sensation (pain) in the body.

Reaction of touching the painful place.

No local sign about the sensation. Any more than a temporal sign about a memory-image. (Temporal signs in a photograph.)

Pain differentiated from other sensations by a characteristic expression. This makes it akin to joy (which is not a sense-experience).

'Sensations give us knowledge of the external world.'

It should be remembered that these are only brief notes of points that Wittgenstein was able to elaborate greatly.[35]

One important element common to the two schemes is the definition of the field of the psychological by reference to the distinctive nature of psychological verbs: a psychological verb is characterized by the fact that whereas the third person present is stated (or is to be verified) on grounds of observation – observation of behaviour – the first person present is not. It is in accordance with this characterization that I do not say what I am thinking about, or visualising, or what emotion or sensation I am experiencing, on the basis of observation of anything at all, but if you say what I am thinking about or visualising, or what emotion or sensation I am experiencing, you will say or establish this on the basis of observation, and in particular observation of my behaviour. Now it is true that there is an inclination to water down this point, and to concede that although I do not learn what I can say about my present thoughts, images, emotions, or sensations by means of observation of my behaviour, the reason for this is that whereas others are restricted to whatever can be observed of the effects of my mental events on my bodily appearance and behaviour, I can observe the contents of my mind directly. Hence the asymmetry between the first person and the third person is to be explained by reference to the different points of view from which the inner life can be observed: from an external point of view it is hidden and can be detected only indirectly, but from the point of view of the subject himself it is directly visible. Wittgenstein argues, however, that this is a misconstruction of the grammar of psychological verbs and that I do not report the observation of anything when I give verbal expression to my present thoughts, images, emotions, or sensations. The asymmetry between the first person and the third person is therefore not to be explained by reference to the different kinds of observational access open to the two points of view.

This point is emphasised in the second classificatory scheme, where the initial characterization of psychological verbs is immediately followed by an additional description of utterances of the two kinds, which introduces a distinctive feature of Wittgenstein's later philosophy of psychology:

> Sentences in the third person present: information. In the first person present: expression. ((Not quite right.))
> The first person of the present akin to an expression.[36]

This is Wittgenstein's expressive account of first person present psychological utterances, which likens them to the natural, non-linguistic expression of psychological states and places them at a distance from the use of sentences to transmit information that has been acquired by the person who utters them. I develop

Wittgenstein's account in the examination of his investigation of sensation-language in chapter III.

A second important element common to the two schemes is the use of the idea of a certain kind (or sense) of duration to identify and distinguish psychological categories. Wittgenstein often referred to this as *genuine* duration and he used the idea to characterize the difference between 'states of consciousness', sensations, sense-impressions and images, for example, and psychological 'dispositions' (and capacities), such as knowledge, belief, understanding and intention.[37] Thus the first scheme for the classification of psychological concepts divides the field of the psychological in the manner represented by this tree-diagram:

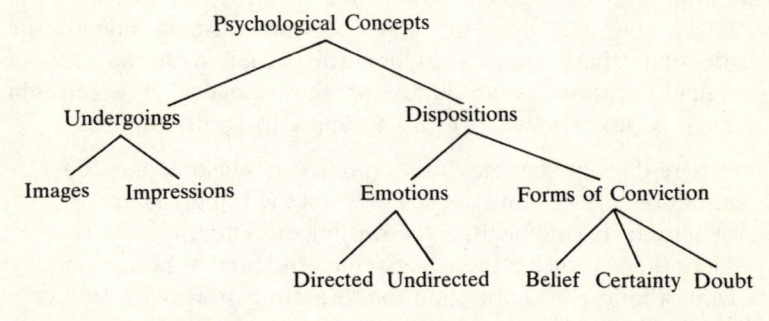

And one criterion for inclusion in the class of undergoings is that the item should possess a certain kind of duration (genuine duration). Likewise, the second scheme characterizes both sensations and emotions in terms of genuine duration (which also applies to the third element of the scheme, images).[38]

What is the concept of genuine duration, and can it be used to distinguish the concept of a state of consciousness from such concepts as knowledge, belief, understanding, and intention?

Wittgenstein explained the concept of genuine duration in a number of interconnected ways. If something has genuine duration:

(1) It has a temporal structure, a uniform or non-uniform course.[39]

(2) It is possible to specify its beginning and end. Hence it is possible that something should occur simultaneously with it and the two occurrences be synchronized.[40]

(3) One can ascertain by spot-checking that it is going on.[41]
(4) Its duration can be determined by means of a stop-watch.[42]
(5) It is interrupted by (a) a break in consciousness (sleep, for example), or (b) withdrawal of attention from it.[43]
(6) It is possible to follow its temporal course with attention.[44]
(7) It makes sense to speak of it as having endured continuously from one time until another.[45]
(8) There is such a thing as uninterrupted observation of its duration.[46]

Can the class of sensations, sense-impressions, and images be characterized, at least in part, by the common possession of this set of properties, and do knowledge, belief, understanding and intention each lack all, most or some of these features?

If we consider, first, the state of consciousness side of the distinction, there appears to be little wrong with the idea of genuine duration as an index of the category. Wittgenstein himself points out that (6) fails to apply to mental images:

> Where there is genuine duration one can tell someone: 'Pay attention and give me the signal when the thing you are experiencing (the picture, the rattling etc.) alters.'
> Here there *is* such a thing as paying attention. Whereas one cannot follow with attention the forgetting of what one knew or the like.
> [Not right, for one also cannot follow one's own mental images with attention.][47]

And if one cannot follow one's mental images with attention, then also one cannot withdraw one's attention from them, so that (5b) fails to apply. Furthermore, (8) appears to be a mere reformulation of (6). We must therefore delete these from the list. What remains captures the class of sensations, sense-impressions, and images.

But when we turn to the other side of the distinction, the situation is not so straightforward. (4) certainly applies to a belief, or an intention to perform an action, that someone acquires or forms at one time and then gives up at a later time when something happens to make him change his mind: the moment at which the belief or intention is formed and the moment at which it changes could be recorded by a stop-watch. Likewise, (2) applies to such a belief or such an intention (unless

14

the idea of synchronization requires more than the correlation of beginning and end points). On the other hand, knowledge that, knowledge how and understanding are abilities; a person's beliefs about his abilities are not infallible; and the duration of an ability is determined by tests. Hence these psychological dispositions fail to satisfy (4). Wittgenstein assigned pride of place to (3), but it is easy to ascertain by spot-check whether one still believes that Mozart died in 1791 or still intends to visit Rome next April. It is not clear exactly what (1) demands. Perhaps it requires only that an item should possess a dimension along which it can vary while retaining its identity. So a person's toothache is something that has genuine duration, since it remains toothache through fluctuations in its intensity. If we regard belief as an all-or-nothing notion, then belief fails to satisfy the demands of (1), because a belief is defined by its propositional content and lacks the required variable property. But desire can certainly vary in strength and would fall on the dispositional side of the state of consciousness/disposition divide. Moreover, the intention to perform a certain action is subject to changes in its determinate content, as when one's intention to visit Rome in April endures but one now intends to travel by car, not aeroplane, or with Jill, not Jack.[48] And there is a final point: (5a) appears to use the notion of a state of consciousness, and so could not be used to explicate the notion without circularity.

The result is that if there is to be a single criterion for genuine duration, and the idea of genuine duration is to be a self-sufficient mark of the distinction between states of consciousness and psychological dispositions, the weight must fall on (7). It is unclear whether so slight a linguistic indication can bear such weight; it is uncertain, however, whether Wittgenstein intended it to.

PSYCHOLOGICAL CONCEPTS, PRIVACY, AND BEHAVIOUR

We have already encountered two distinctive features of Wittgenstein's philosophy of psychology: his expressive account of utterances of first-person present psychological sentences, and the emphasis he places on the heterogeneity of the psychological. This second feature is not restricted to the identification of different kinds of employment within the use of a single psychological word; a more important application is to the uses of different kinds of psychological word. We have seen that Wittgenstein wished to draw a distinction between states of consciousness and dispositional psychological states and we have examined the principal criterion by reference to which he believed the two kinds of state could be differentiated. But this is only one of many distinctions in the roles of words in our psychological vocabulary that must be grasped, Wittgenstein believed, if an adequate reflective understanding of these words is to be achieved. For although states of consciousness are united by the common feature of genuine duration, they exhibit many significant differences; and although dispositional psychological states are bound together by their lack of genuine duration, there are many respects in which they do not resemble one another. Wittgenstein's concern with the elucidation of differences in the grammar of psychological words is apparent in his treatment of the psychological concepts examined in the rest of the book.

I now want to introduce two further characteristic features of Wittgenstein's philosophy of psychology. The first is his opposition to a certain idea of the nature of psychological states (or at least states of consciousness) and his critique of an associated thesis about the way in which words for these psychological states must be learnt. The idea is that states of consciousness are essentially private, or possess an essentially private aspect, in the sense that only the subject of a state of consciousness can ever really know what the intrinsic nature of his state of consciousness is. It follows from this conception that someone can understand which kind of state of consciousness is designated by a psychological word only through being aware in his own case of the nature of the state it is applied to. Hence each person must give himself a 'private ostensive definition' of each kind of state of consciousness designated by a word he understands: when he is in a certain state of consciousness he must direct his attention to it and undertake to use a certain word as the name of states of consciousness of the same kind. And hence also it will be an illusion that there is a common understanding of a name of a state of consciousness, unless each person manages to pick out the same state of consciousness in his private ostensive definition of the word. Wittgenstein attempts to show not only that this is a misunderstanding of the grammar of words for states of consciousness, but that no word could be introduced into a language by the activity of private ostensive definition. His critique of the idea of private ostensive definition is explained in Chapter III.

The second additional feature of Wittgenstein's philosophy of psychology I want to introduce is the all-important role assigned to the idea of behaviour in his account of psychological concepts. We have already seen that Wittgenstein rejected the view that the asymmetry in the use of psychological verbs in the first-person and the third-person present is to be explained as a consequence of the fact that whereas the subject can observe his own psychological states, another person can observe only the subject's behaviour. On the contrary, although the subject's first-person present utterances are not based on observation of his behaviour, it does not follow, and it is in fact false, that they are based on the observation of anything else, something hidden from an external observer's view. Hence there is nothing to be observed other than the subject's behaviour in order to determine whether a psychological predicate applies to him. So the only criteria that can govern the use of psychological words are behaviour-criteria. Furthermore, Wittgenstein argues that any meaningful psychological predicate requires criteria that determine its use, so that something that does not satisfy the criteria for a psychological predicate cannot properly have the predicate ascribed to it. Since these criteria must be behaviour-criteria, we reach the conclusion:

> only of a living human being and what resembles (behaves like) a living human being can one say: it has sensations; it sees; is blind; hears; is deaf; is conscious or unconscious.[49]

Wittgenstein's emphasis on behaviour is also prominent in his remarks about the science of psychology. The psychologist is said to observe and describe the *phenomena* of mental life;[50] and since Wittgenstein meant by 'a phenomenon' something that can be observed,[51] this means that the psychologist observes behaviour (only). It is on this ground that Wittgenstein distinguishes psychology from physics:

> Misleading parallel: psychology treats of processes in the psychical sphere, as does physics in the physical.

17

Seeing, hearing, thinking, feeling, willing, are not the subject of psychology *in the same sense* as that in which the movements of bodies, the phenomena of electricity etc., are the subject of physics. You can see this from the fact that the physicist sees, hears, thinks about, and informs us of these phenomena, and the psychologist observes the *external reactions* (the behaviour) of the subject.[52]

Now it is not my intention to explore this supposed disanalogy between the two sciences, for my purpose here is only to bring out the importance of the role of behaviour in Wittgenstein's thought about psychology and psychological concepts. The importance of this role has in fact often been taken as tantamount to a commitment to some form of behaviourism. But the force of any charge of behaviourism depends on the content of the term. Wittgenstein clearly rejected one conception of behaviourism. If a behaviourist about psychological concepts is someone who insists that the words 'pain', 'joy', 'intention', 'belief', 'thought' stand for forms of behaviour, then Wittgenstein was not a behaviourist.[53] It was precisely this conception of behaviourism that formed one of the two rocks between which Wittgenstein considered the true course in the philosophy of psychology to lie. He thought that we must plot our course between the two extremes of behaviourism and dualism:

> It looks like obscurantism to say that . . . mathematics does not *treat* of signs, or that pain is not a form of behaviour. But only because people believe that one is asserting the existence of an intangible, i.e. a shadowy, object side by side with what we all can grasp. Whereas we are only pointing to different modes of employment of words.[54]

Just as it is wrong to say that '13 + 56 = 69' is about the signs it uses, so it is wrong to say that sentences in which psychological words occur are about behaviour (because such words designate *phenomena*, forms of behaviour). But just as it would be wrong, according to Wittgenstein, to conclude that numbers are an obscure kind of object, so it would be wrong to conclude that psychological states are non-physical 'inner' occurrences. Hence we are presented with a false dichotomy if we are faced with a choice between behaviourism and a Cartesian view of the mind:

18

psychological sentences are used differently from sentences that can be said to be about behaviour, without thereby being used to designate immaterial states. And hence also the fact that psychology observes nothing but behaviour does not imply that psychology deals with behaviour, not the mind. For a subject's utterances of first-person psychological sentences are part of the behaviour psychology observes, and these are not about the subject's behaviour; and descriptions in which observations of behaviour are formulated will typically be couched in psychological terms, and these terms do not designate forms of behaviour.

But this kind of behaviourism is singularly implausible and it is unlikely that Wittgenstein would be thought guilty of it. There is, however, a more sophisticated form of behaviourism than this simple kind, which does not involve an identification of psychological events with forms of behaviour, that is present in Wittgenstein's writings about the philosophy of psychology and that explains the repeated charge of behaviourism brought against his account of psychological concepts. For Wittgenstein denies that the words 'see', 'visualise', 'pain', 'intention', 'joy', 'belief', and so on, stand for states, events or processes that cause the behaviour in which seeing, visual imagining, pain, intention, joy and belief are manifested. It is this aspect of his view that renders his treatment of psychological concepts problematic. The idea that the true course in the philosophy of psychology lies between behaviourism and dualism is familiar. But what is normally thought to lie between these two extremes is some form of materialism, in accordance with which psychological states (or at least their non-relational cores) are conceived as internal physical events lying behind behaviour and bringing it about. An account of psychological concepts that denies the foundations of any materialistic view of psychological states and events by rejecting the assumption that psychological predicates designate states or events that stand in a causal relation to the behaviour that indicates the applicability of the predicates, is both unfamiliar and a novel form of behaviourism. Whether it is viable is a matter for investigation.

MYTHICAL STATES OF CONSCIOUSNESS

The idea of the essential privacy of psychological states has many roots. This is especially true in the case of states of consciousness. But there is one important pattern of thought identified by Wittgenstein that does not apply to states of consciousness. It consists in *wrongly construing* a psychological expression as standing for a state of consciousness, and then, because no description of the state seems adequate, concluding that the expression stands for something that cannot be described and that must be experienced if the expression designating it is to be understood. Since the meaning of the expression is not captured by a description of what happens in someone's consciousness when the expression begins to apply to him, if we misconstrue the expression as standing for a state of consciousness we will be misled into thinking that it stands for a specific, indefinable experience.[55] We have seen that Wittgenstein's aim in his treatment of psychological concepts is to create a perspicuous representation of the meanings of psychological words, the ways in which they are used, as a prophylactic against philosophical confusions about the mind. A precondition of success in this enterprise is a secure grasp of the relation between the concepts of understanding and meaning words in a certain way and the psychological states and processes that are experienced by people when they use and understand language. I outline Wittgenstein's conception of this relation, and also the essence of his consideration of the concept of following a rule, in the next chapter. It will be seen that the expression 'sudden understanding', which Wittgenstein highlights, is just such an expression for which the pattern of thought I have mentioned is a temptation.

II

CONSCIOUSNESS AND THE UNDERSTANDING OF LANGUAGE

PRESENCE AND ABSENCE

Wittgenstein's conception of the meaning of a word is encapsulated by his dictum that the meaning of a word is its use in the language.[1] But there is an apparent tension between this conception and the undeniable fact that we understand the meaning of a word when we hear or say it. When I hear a word and understand what it means or when I utter the word with that meaning can the whole use of the word come before my mind? How could the use of the word in the language be condensed into something that might come before my mind in an instant? But then if it could not, how could I give that meaning to it or understand it in that sense at that very moment of time?

Now this is an instance of a more general problem, which concerns the relation between what is present and what is not present, what takes place at a certain time and what does not take place at that time, what is present in someone's mind at a certain time and what, so it seems, is not present there. Wittgenstein's concern with a variety of instances of this general problem has a particular focus: it is concentrated upon what is present *to* or *before* someone's mind, in the sense in which something can be said to be present to or before someone's mind when something happens that the person experiences or performs and of which he is aware. The problem can be expressed in this way: How can what is present to someone's mind 'contain' what is not present – as it seems to do when the person is truly described at the time in terms that refer to what is not present? Or instead: What is the relation between a person and what is not present when he is correctly described at a time when something is present to his mind by a predicate that imports a reference to what is not present? Thus if the occasion when something happens to a person's mind (i.e., something is present to his mind) is one when he can be said to have grasped in a flash the meaning of a word, to have meant a mathematical formula a certain way, to have realised how to continue a series of numbers, to have recalled how a tune goes (without hearing it through), to have decided to play chess, what is the relation between what happened in the person's mind and the predicates 'grasped (in a flash) the meaning of the word', 'meant the formula this way', 'realised how to continue the series', 'recalled how the tune goes', 'decided to play chess'? Each of these predicates imports a reference to what is not present (an absent 'object'): the use of the word, the series of numbers, the tune in its entirety, the totality of rules that determines the game of chess. And suddenly one of these predicates can truly be ascribed to a person, when a moment before it could not. What is the relation between this fact and whatever, at that moment, happens in, comes before or becomes present to, the person's mind?

THE EXTRINSIC AND INTRINSIC CONCEPTIONS OF THE FICTITIOUS STATE OF CONSCIOUSNESS

In all these cases, so Wittgenstein thought, there is a strong temptation to construe the predicate as standing for a specific state of consciousness or a particular conscious process: a state or process in which something is present to a person's mind. The state (or process) of consciousness for which the predicate supposedly stands can be thought of in two different ways. It might be thought of as a state of consciousness whose nature can be fully specified without explicit or implicit reference to the absent 'object' referred to by the predicate. This can be called the extrinsic conception of the state of consciousness. Alternatively, it might be thought of as a state of consciousness whose intrinsic character 'contains' the (seemingly) absent 'object'. This is the intrinsic conception. According to the extrinsic conception, the relation between the state of consciousness and its 'object' is an external relation; according to the intrinsic conception the relation is internal.

Now if the state of consciousness is thought of in the extrinsic way, two difficulties immediately present themselves. In the first place, the presence of the state of consciousness is neither a logically necessary nor a logically sufficient condition for the predicate to apply. Consider, for example, someone who suddenly realises how to continue a series of numbers. When he suddenly understands how to continue the series various conscious processes may take place in his mind. Perhaps what comes before his mind is a formula (which yields the initial segment of the series when applied in the standard fashion). But to say that someone has suddenly understood how to continue a series is neither to say nor to imply that he has thought of a particular formula, or even of any formula; and someone who thinks of a formula may not have understood how to continue the series, no matter what formula it is. A similar conclusion holds for each of the conscious processes that may have occurred at the time the person realised how to continue the series: no such conscious process guarantees understanding, and understanding does not require any particular one of these processes.

The second difficulty for the extrinsic conception of the state of consciousness that is supposedly signified by the predicate concerns the connection between the state of consciousness and the absent 'object' by reference to which the predicate characterises the state of consciousness. What is this connection? Why is *this* state of consciousness – a state of consciousness whose intrinsic nature can be fully specified without reference to the absent 'object' – designated by *this* predicate – a predicate that refers to the 'object'? It seems that the connection would have to be something of this kind: the state of consciousness has been found to be correlated in some way with the ability or activity that is relevantly connected with the absent 'object'. So the predicate 'decided to play chess' stands for a certain state of consciousness because it has been discovered that when someone is in that state of consciousness this is often followed by his playing a game of chess, rather than something else or nothing at all. And the predicate 'recalled how the tune goes' stands for a different state of consciousness because someone who is in this state of consciousness often proceeds to reproduce the tune without aids. But if the connection between the state of consciousness and its absent 'object' (the game, the tune) is in this sense only a matter of experience, it will make sense to ask someone who is in this state whether he is certain, and how he knows, that his state is directed to that 'object'. It will not be possible for someone to specify the 'object' by simply attending to his state of consciousness and reading it off the state, because the 'object' is not included in the intrinsic character of the state. Yet the question 'How do I know I want to play chess?' makes no sense if I know which game chess is. And it would be nonsense for me to say that I don't know whether my desire is the desire to play chess or to do something quite different. Accordingly, if the state of consciousness is related to its 'object' only in this external way, a person's awareness of what he wants to do is rendered problematic and nonsensical sentences are rendered meaningful.

For these reasons the intrinsic conception of the state of consciousness for which a predicate of the class under consideration is supposed to stand is more attractive than the extrinsic conception. The difficulties that the extrinsic conception faces are reduced if the state of consciousness is conceived differently, as containing its 'object', which was only apparently absent from the mind. If there is a state of consciousness that contains the game of chess – the rules that are definitive of the game – then I can read off from the state which game it is that I want to play. And unless there is such a state of consciousness, how can I know what I want to do: if what I want to do is not present in my consciousness, how can I know that it is *this* that I want to do? Hence there is some plausibility in the suggestion that the presence of this state of consciousness is both a logically necessary and a logically sufficient condition for someone to have decided to play a game of chess. Likewise, when I suddenly remember how a tune goes, without singing it through aloud or in the head, it can seem plausible to say 'In some sense it was there in its entirety at the moment' and to postulate a queer state or process which my suddenly knowing how the tune goes consists in – the tune flashes through my mind in an instant.

But this plausibility rapidly disappears when the conception of such an instantaneous state of consciousness or such a momentary process is scrutinised. It is untrue that whenever I decide to play a game of chess the rules of the game pass in extraordinarily rapid succession through my mind. And even if on some occasion this were to happen, these rules would be mere expressions or signs and so would not guarantee the nature of my decision – any more than the presence of a formula before my mind guarantees that I have understood how to continue a series of numbers that can be generated by the formula. Furthermore, the mythical nature of the state of consciousness required by the intrinsic conception becomes readily apparent if we consider the case of someone who suddenly realises how to continue a series of numbers or who intends a formula for developing a series to be understood in a certain way. If the postulated state of consciousness is to guarantee that the person understands how to continue the series or that he intended the formula to be understood in a certain way, it must contain each of the members of the series that he has understood how to continue or that he intended to be developed. And the difficulty in seeing how this can be so – for the series has infinitely many members – underlies the view that understanding and intention are states of consciousness that are indescribable.[2]

However, the temptation to postulate such a queer state or process arises only if the expression '(suddenly) understanding how to continue the series' is construed as standing for a current state of a person's consciousness or a conscious process that occurs when he understands how to go on. If we do this 'We interpret the enigma created by our misunderstanding as the enigma of an incomprehensible process'.[3] The moral that Wittgenstein draws is that this is a misconstrual: understanding is not a state or process that consists in something's being present to a person's mind. And, more generally, in the case of each member of the class of predicates we are considering Wittgenstein reaches the same negative conclusion: the concept of the kind of thing signified by the predicate is not the concept of any particular event or process that takes place in a person's mind when the predicate becomes true of him. The predicate does not stand for some happening in his consciousness. It is unsurprising that there are many direct statements in Wittgenstein's writings of the conclusion that a person's intention or what he means by

25

the words he utters is not a state of consciousness, since it was specially important for him to establish the point in the case of the concepts of meaning and intention.[4]

It follows that the condition of someone who suddenly understands how to continue a series of numbers need not be distinguished from that of someone who does not, or his own condition before he understood, by something that was present to or went through his mind but was not present to or did not go through the mind of the other person, or his own mind before he understood. And a similar conclusion can be drawn for the other mental concepts that Wittgenstein considers.

DISPOSITIONS AND MENTAL MECHANISMS

Although Wittgenstein's concern with the various instances of the general problem of the relation between what is and what is not present is predominantly to do with what is present *to* or *before* a person's mind, this is not always so. In two places in *Philosophical Investigations* he considers a different sense in which something might be said to be present *in* someone's mind or a present state *of* his mind, and in this sense what is present is not a state of consciousness. The view that Wittgenstein puts forward is essentially the same in the two cases.

The first case concerns the suggestion that knowing which series is to be developed in accordance with a certain formula is like knowing the alphabet. Wittgenstein replies to the suggestion in this way:

> If one says that knowing the ABC is a state of mind, one is thinking of a state of a mental apparatus (perhaps of the brain) by means of which we explain the *manifestations* of that knowledge. Such a state is called a disposition. But there are objections to speaking of a state of the mind here, inasmuch as there ought to be two different criteria for such a state: a knowledge of the construction of the apparatus, quite apart from what it does.[5]

Now the objection Wittgenstein refers to is an objection to saying that knowledge of the alphabet is a state of a *mental apparatus*: it is not an objection to saying that it is a *state (of a person).*[6]

Furthermore, this idea of a mental apparatus is not the one that is sometimes his target: he is not here attacking the idea of a 'purely mental' apparatus, one that is not made of matter and that can bring about effects no material mechanism could achieve.[7] The objection is directed against the view that someone who possesses such a capacity as knowledge of the alphabet must have a mental apparatus, some state of which is the causal foundation of the capacity and so explains its manifestations.[8] But the objection is unconvincing. It is true that I do not find out that I have the capacity by finding out that my mental apparatus is in a certain state, nor do others find this out about me by this method. Moreover, knowledge of the construction of my mental apparatus that is not knowledge of the functions it enables me to perform will not be sufficient to determine whether I know the alphabet. For it is not the fact that my mental apparatus satisfies a certain physical description, but the fact that it is this state of my mental apparatus that enables me to reproduce the alphabet without aids, that entitles us to say that my knowledge of the alphabet is founded in this state of my mental apparatus. It is also true that the capacity could be differently based in different people, or in the same person at different times: possession of the same capacity does not require a mental apparatus constructed in an identical fashion. But this does not imply that it is coherent to suggest that the capacity might be possessed by someone who lacks a mental apparatus in which the capacity is based. Wittgenstein appears to be relying upon the supposition that if there is a single criterion for the possession of a psychological capacity, and this criterion makes no reference to a mental apparatus in which the capacity is founded, then it cannot be an *a priori* requirement that possession of the capacity must be founded in a mental apparatus.

This supposition is clearly at work on the second occasion when Wittgenstein engages with a more generous sense of what is present in a person's mind. This occurs in his discussion of so-called 'reading'. By 'reading' Wittgenstein understands the ability to follow certain kinds of rule: the ability to transpose written or printed words into speech, spoken words into written, a score into sounds, and so on. He asks us to consider what the difference is between someone who can read and a beginner who is only pretending to read at a time when each utters the same word, and also the case of a pupil who is being trained to be used as a reading-machine and changes from not being able to read to being able to do so. Wittgenstein replies to the suggestion that there must be a difference between what happens in the practised reader and what happens in the beginner who is pretending to read, if not in what they are conscious of at least in the mechanisms at work (perhaps in their brains), by saying that 'these mechanisms are only hypotheses, models designed to explain, to sum up, what you observe'.[9] And he makes a similar point about the change in the pupil who becomes a living reading-machine. Wittgenstein rejects the idea that there must be a first word that the pupil actually reads and maintains that because *'reading' just means reacting to written signs in such-and-such ways*, the concept of reading is 'quite independent of that of a mental or other mechanism'.[10] And he follows this with a series of questions designed to undermine the insistence that there must be a mechanism in the pupil which enables him to read and by reference to which it can be determined when he begins to read.

Wittgenstein's thinking is illuminated here by an illustration of which he was fond:

> Think of two different kinds of plant, A and B, both of which yield seeds; the seeds of both kinds look exactly the same and even after the most careful investigation we can find no difference between them. But the seeds of an A-plant always produce more A-plants, the seeds of a B-plant, more B-plants. In this situation we can predict what sort of plant will grow out of such a seed only if we know which plant it has come from. – Are we to be satisfied with this; or should we say: 'There *must* be a difference in the seeds themselves, otherwise they *couldn't* produce different plants; their previous histories on their own *can't* cause their further development unless their histories have left traces in the seeds themselves.'?
>
> And to protest: 'There must be a difference in the seeds, even if we don't discover it', doesn't alter the facts, it only shows what a powerful urge we have to see everything in terms of cause and effect.
>   When people talk about graphology, physiognomics and such-like they constantly say: '. . . clearly character must be

expressed in handwriting *somehow* . . .' 'Must': that means we are going to apply this picture come what may.[11]

This example of the seeds throws light on two of Wittgenstein's attitudes: his attitude towards the possibility of explaining human behaviour by reference to what happens in people's bodies and his attitude towards counter-factual conditionals. I will consider each attitude in turn.

In *Zettel* the example of the seeds is described in such a way that it is laid down that *there is no difference* in the two kinds of seed, other than their histories, that corresponds with the difference in the plants that result from them. The example is sandwiched between:

> No supposition seems to me more natural than that there is no
> process in the brain correlated with associating or with
> thinking; so that it would be impossible to read off thought-
> processes from brain-processes. I mean this: if I talk or write
> there is, I assume, a system of impulses going out from my
> brain and correlated with my spoken or written thoughts. But
> why should the *system* continue further in the direction of the
> centre? Why should this order not proceed, so to speak, out of
> chaos? The case would be like the following –

and:

> So an organism might come into being even out of something
> quite amorphous, as it were causelessly; and there is no reason
> why this should not really hold for our thoughts, and hence for
> our thinking and writing.[12]

The moral is clear. Wittgenstein is claiming that it is conceivable that the causal chains inside a person's body that bring about the bodily movements in which his thoughts are expressed might terminate in chaos. The implication for the case of the practised reader and the beginner who is only pretending to read is that it is possible that there is no relevant difference in what happens in their bodies, for there does not need to be a mechanism in the body of the practised reader that explains his ability to read. Similarly, the transition of the potential living reading-machine from the condition of not being able to read to possession of the ability need not involve a change in his body that would allow the acquisition of this ability to be explained by reference to a new mechanism within the body or a modification of an old mechanism: the concept of reading is 'quite independent of that of a mental or other mechanism'.

That this is the correct interpretation of Wittgenstein's remarks is confirmed by what he writes about memory. The view he puts forward is that when he remembers the name of someone whom he had seen long ago and has now seen again there need not be a cause of this remembering in his nervous system: the concept of memory does not require that when he remembers the person's name his body is in a condition that is a result of his previous experience of the person.[13] Wittgenstein rejects the insistence that there must be a physiological foundation of the ability to remember as a fruit of a primitive interpretation of the concept of memory and embraces the possibility of a causal relation between psychological phenomena which is not mediated physiologically.[14] The point I wish to extract from this view is Wittgenstein's commitment to the possibility that there could be two people, with no (relevant) physical difference between the conditions of their bodies at a certain time, one of whom can and does remember something at that time, the other of whom cannot remember that thing. This is the memory analogue of Wittgenstein's seeds. Consider two of these seeds, one of which has come from a plant of kind A and the other from a plant of kind B. Suppose that both seeds fail to germinate because of lack of water. It will then be true to say of one seed that if it had been watered it would have become a plant of kind A, and of the other that if it had been watered it would have become a plant of kind B. And these different counter-factual conditionals will be true despite the fact that there is no intrinsic, non-relational difference between the physical states of the two seeds and no difference in their circumstances. Similarly, Wittgenstein wishes to allow that different counter-factual conditionals could be true of people in the same circumstances, without the difference being dependent upon a physical difference in the conditions of the people's bodies.

MEANING AND COUNTER-FACTUAL CONDITIONALS

The significance of Wittgenstein's supposition that psychological differences need not be based in physical differences and counter-factual differences need not be based in intrinsic, non-relational differences derives from the positive account that he sketches of such concepts as meaning, intention and understanding. In his consideration of someone who orders a pupil to write down the series given by the order '+2', Wittgenstein readily concedes that the person can be said to have known, at the time he gave the order, that the pupil ought to write 1002 after 1000; he can be said to have *meant* him to do this, even though he did not think of this step at the time. The misconception Wittgenstein opposes is that if the person meant him to do this then a conscious process took place in his mind that determined that this was the step to be taken at this point of the series; and, similarly, for each step he did not think of at the time, but at the time meant, it determined that this was the step to be taken at that point of the series. But if we reject the idea of the process in the mind that contains all the intended steps, what account should be given of the statement that the person meant the pupil to write 1002 after 1000? Wittgenstein's answer is that the sentence 'I already knew, at the time when I gave the order, that he ought to write 1002 after 1000', or the sentence 'I meant him to write 1002 after 1000', *means something like* 'If I had then been asked what number should be written after 1000, I should have replied "1002"'.[15] Again, he says that the past tense of the word 'mean' in the sentence 'I meant you to write . . .' can be explained by putting the sentence into the form 'Had you asked me before what I wanted you to do at this stage, I should have said. . .'.[16] And Wittgenstein does not doubt that it might be true of someone that he would have given a certain answer if he had then been asked. The point he proceeds to make is that when someone declares what reply he would have given to a question if he had been asked it, what he says is an assumption or hypothesis. It is an hypothesis that he would have made that reply, and the person's supposition that he would have said this is of a similar kind to the one made by someone who says 'If he had fallen into the water then, I should have jumped in after him'.

And Wittgenstein makes this point not to call into question that a person can be said to know that he intended his words to be construed in a certain way, but rather to emphasise that what someone means by his words is not determined by what happens before his mind when he utters them. Although someone can properly be said to recall what he meant by the words he uttered on a certain occasion, what he thereby recalls is not a state of consciousness but is comparable to the truth of a counter-factual conditional.

Now Wittgenstein's reference to a certain kind of counter-factual conditional is only intended to indicate in a rough manner the sort of meaning that such a sentence as 'I meant him to write 1002 after 1000' has. It would be mistaken to construe him as proposing a counter-factual *analysis* of sentences of this kind. Nevertheless, it is clear that Wittgenstein believed that the understanding of counter-factual conditionals is integral to an understanding of the class of concepts under consideration – in particular, to the concepts of meaning, intention, understanding, and knowledge. And we have seen reason to suppose that he did not require that if a counter-factual conditional that expresses what someone would have said if he had been asked a certain question is true of one person but not of another, then there must be some difference between the mental apparatuses of the two people that accounts for this fact. Neither did he require that each of these conditionals that is true of a person at a given time must be true in virtue of the current state of his mental apparatus. For if each of the person's counter-factual remarks, had it been spoken, might have been at one end of a causal chain the other end of which terminates inside the person's body in chaos, the truth of no one of the counter-factual conditionals could require that the current state of his mental apparatus should be part of what makes it true.

THE CONSTITUTION OF MEANING

If this interpretation of Wittgenstein is correct, then we can reach the following conclusion. Wittgenstein's thesis is that the condition of someone who suddenly understands how to continue a series need not be distinguished from that of someone who does not understand, or his own condition before he understood, either by (i) something that was present to or went through his mind but which was not present to or did not go through the mind of the other person, or his own before he understood or by (ii) the condition of his mental apparatus. And parallel conclusions can be drawn for the other 'mental phenomena' Wittgenstein considers: grasping the meaning of a word (in a flash), intending a formula a certain way, recalling the way a tune goes (without running right through it), deciding to play chess. These 'mental phenomena', according to Wittgenstein, can therefore be said not to consist in or be composed of anything at all: anything that happens to a person or that the person does. When it becomes true to say of a person that he has understood the meaning of a word, for example, neither the state of his consciousness nor the state of his mental apparatus is required, by the concept of understanding, to have changed in some way. And when someone means something by the words he utters, no contemporaneous occurrence will constitute his meaning that thing:

> The mistake is to say that there is anything that meaning
> something consists in.[17]

THE TWO THEMES

There are therefore two themes in Wittgenstein's discussion of the class of predicates under consideration. One theme is that a predicate of this class does not signify a process or state of consciousness. The other theme is that the application of such a predicate does not presuppose that the subject of the predicate has a mental apparatus which operates in a law-governed manner to produce the movements of his body in which the 'mental phenomenon' signified by the predicate is expressed. In particular, the notion of what a person means does not impose the requirement that someone who means something should possess a mental apparatus the condition of which reflects what he means; and so it does not require that a person's ability to master a language should be causally explicable by reference to the nature of his mental apparatus. However, it is clear that this second theme is subsidiary. It takes up little space in Wittgenstein's work, and it was not integral to his chief concerns to establish that the necessity of a certain kind of causal explanation of the ability to use language is not inherent in the concept of language. Wittgenstein was concerned to stress not so much the supposed fact that the causal chains inside a person's body may come to an end in chaos but that the giving of reasons comes to an end. And the fact that the chain of reasons comes to an end is connected with Wittgenstein's main theme: a predicate of the class under consideration does not signify a process or state of consciousness.

I now want to put aside Wittgenstein's view that it is inessential that a language-user should have a mental apparatus in which his understanding of language is founded and to consider instead his opposition to a rationalistic account of the understanding and use of language. This takes us to the heart of Wittgenstein's consideration of rule-following.

MEANING AND INTERPRETATION

We have already seen that understanding a sign is not a state or process that consists in something's being present to a person's mind. How, if at all, someone understands a sign is not determined by what he has before his mind. Hence hearing a sign with understanding does not require the presence before the person's mind of something other than the sign itself, this additional item making it true that he understands the sign in a certain way. The temptation to believe that the sign needs an accompaniment is motivated in part by the realisation that someone can hear a sign with or without understanding. Therefore the mere *fact* that the sign is present to the mind is insufficient for understanding to take place. Hence it can seem as if something must be added to the sign if the sign is to be understood: to understand a sign something more must be present to the mind than just the sign itself. But whatever accompanied the sign, Wittgenstein writes, 'would for us just be another sign'.[18] If we call the substitution of one sign for another, or the addition of one sign to another, an interpretation of the sign, and the sign substituted or added an interpretation of the original sign, then the thought is that not merely must the sign that is understood be present to the mind but so must an interpretation of the sign.[19] But since an interpretation is just another sign, the presence to the mind of the sign and an interpretation is logically on a par with the presence of just the sign itself. Just as the original sign can be variously interpreted, so can any interpretation of the sign. Hence it is not a requirement of hearing a sign with understanding that the sign should be interpreted: an interpretation yields only something of the same nature as the original sign, and an interpretation does not determine what, if anything, the sign is taken to mean. And what holds for hearing a sign with understanding will hold for all understanding of signs, and in particular for all understanding, and all meaningful uses, of language:

> The meaning of a phrase for us is characterised by the use we make of it. The meaning is not a mental accompaniment to the expression.[20]

Why would anything that accompanied a sign just be another sign and so an interpretation of the sign? The reason should now be clear. Anything that *could* be present to someone's mind in addition to the sign he is using or perceiving and that might be appealed to as establishing that he understood the sign in a certain way will have an intrinsic nature from which it will not follow that this is what he understood the sign to mean. Just as a state of consciousness that consists in the presence before the mind of a sign cannot contain the meaning the person assigns to the sign, neither can a state of consciousness that consists in the presence before the mind of a sign and something else: understanding is not a state of consciousness. Hence Wittgenstein's argument about the irrelevance of mental accompaniments to a sign (i.e., interpretations of the sign) can be seen to be merely a reworking of his familiar point that any ostensive definition can be variously interpreted (i.e., understood);[21] it is unfortunate that he uses the notion of interpretation in an equivocal fashion.

Now mastery of a language involves the ability to use signs in rule-governed ways. Someone understands a sign in a language he has mastered only if he can use it in a rule-governed manner, and when he uses the sign he uses it meaningfully only if he is following a rule. But if he uses the sign meaningfully on some occasion, and his action is therefore an instance of following a rule, what makes this true is not that he has given the sign an interpretation on that occasion: it is not any mental accompaniment to the sign he uses that determines whether he is following a rule on that occasion and, if so, what rule he is following. The failure to recognise this fact gives rise to the paradox that no course of action can be determined by a rule because every course of action can be made out to accord with the rule.[22] For if it were the nature of the mental accompaniment to the use of a sign on a certain occasion that determined whether a particular rule was then being followed, then any action, if accompanied by the right interpretation of the sign, would be a case of following that rule. But, as Wittgenstein observes, if everything can be made out to accord with the rule then it can also be made out to conflict with it – so there would be neither accord nor conflict. For any action, if accompanied by the wrong interpretation, would thereby fail to be a case of following the rule in question. And the point of Wittgenstein's remarks is to draw attention to the fact that although it is always possible to substitute one expression of a rule for another expression or to add one sign to another, no expression of a rule will itself help us to understand what is involved in the idea of someone's following a rule. Therefore, advancing from one expression of a rule to another is no help to this end. It might be thought that someone can understand a rule only if he gives it a particular interpretation. But if 'an interpretation' means the substitution of one expression of the rule for another,[23] the thought is confused. The difficulty that is felt about the person's understanding the original rule will arise equally about his understanding any interpretation he may give to it. Although the expression of a rule is susceptible of different interpretations, any interpretation is itself susceptible of different interpretations. Wittgenstein makes the point in *Philosophical Grammar* like this:

> But an interpretation is something that is given in signs . . . So if one were to say 'Any sentence still stands in need of an interpretation' that would mean: no sentence can be understood without a rider.[24]

The negative conclusion of Wittgenstein's discussion of the concept of following a rule and of his defence of the thesis that the meaning of a word is the use we make of it, is that an interpretation does not determine meaning. This conclusion is drawn explicitly:

> 'But how can a rule shew me what I have to do at *this* point? Whatever I do is, on some interpretation, in accord with the rule.' – That is not what we ought to say, but rather: any interpretation still hangs in the air along with what it interprets, and cannot give it any support. Interpretations by themselves do not determine meaning.[25]

How, if at all, someone understands a rule is not determined by any interpretation he gives the rule.

MEANING, CAPACITY, AND PRACTICE

The positive conclusion of Wittgenstein's consideration of rule-following is:

> there is a way of grasping a rule which is *not* an *interpretation*, but which is exhibited in what we call 'obeying the rule' and 'going against it' in actual cases.[26]

This is, as we should expect, intimately connected with the dissolution of the apparent tension between the dictum that the meaning of a word is its use in the language and the fact that on any occasion when we understand the meaning of a word we speak or hear, the use is not present. And it is also connected with the resolution of the general problem of the absent 'object', of which this apparent tension is an instance. Each member of the problematic class of predicates that Wittgenstein considers requires its subject to possess a capacity: the capacity to make use of a word in a certain way, to continue a series, to reproduce a tune, to play a game. And whether on a certain occasion someone has the required capacity is not determined by whether the relevant absent 'object' is then present to his mind. So the totality of rules of chess need not be present to his mind if he then decides to play chess; the entire tune need not be present to his mind if he then understands how to continue a segment of it or to develop it in accordance with a formula or an order; the use of a word need not be present to his mind if he then understands an instance of it. As a near approximation, a predicate of the problematic class suddenly applies to someone if he then acquires a certain capacity or disposition or the conditions for the realisation of a capacity are then satisfied.[27] Thus someone remembers a tune at a certain moment if he can then spontaneously reproduce it when a moment before he could not; and he suddenly understands how to continue a series if he then acquires the capacity to continue it.[28]

Now a capacity or disposition, unlike an interpretation, is not an accompaniment of a sign.[29] Meaning is determined not by an interpretation, an accompaniment of a sign, but by the way a person is disposed to use or respond to the sign. The 'way of grasping a rule which is *not* an *interpretation*, but which is exhibited in what we call "obeying the rule" and "going against it" in actual cases' is the possession or acquisition of a capacity or disposition to act in a certain way. I grasp the rule for developing a series if I have the ability to develop the series from the rule. My understanding of sign-posts is manifested in how I respond to them on the various occasions I encounter them with, for example, a destination in mind. I understand a word if I can make use of it in a certain way: if I am master of a technique.[30]

If meaning were determined by an interpretation, two things would be true. Firstly, it would be *what happens on an occasion* that determines whether or how on that occasion a sign is meant or understood. But since meaning is not an accompaniment of a sign it is not a matter of what happens when a sign is used or perceived with understanding that endows the sign with its meaning on that occasion. Wittgenstein dramatises this fact by denying that it is possible that there should have been only one occasion on which any sign was ever used to mean something or any rule was ever obeyed.[31]

The second, and related, thing that would be true if an interpretation determined meaning is that someone might mean or understand something by a sign *no matter how he was inclined to use it on other occasions*: meaning would be divorced from use. But understanding a sign is knowing how it is used or how to use it; and how someone understands a sign is therefore determined by the use he is inclined to make of it. If what someone means by a sign were determined by what is present to his mind when he uses it, then no constraints would be imposed on his use of the

38

sign by what he means, or on how he understands the sign by the way in which he uses it. For even if there is no discernible regularity in what he does, he would be deemed to be following a rule in his use of the sign *on a series of occasions* if on each occasion of use what is present to his mind is the same. Regularity in the application of the sign is not required, since regularity in what comes before the mind is sufficient. Furthermore, it would be sufficient for someone to be following a rule in his use of a sign *on a single occasion* if something were then to be before his mind. But these conditions demand nothing since they will always be satisfied: on any occasion of use the sign itself will be present to the person's mind. And if a person's awareness that he has something before his mind on an occasion were sufficient for him to be following a rule, then his thinking he is following a rule (because he has something before his mind) would guarantee that he is following a rule. But if we reject the idea that following a rule is a matter of what is present to a person's mind, and accept that it is instead a matter of there being regularity in what he *does* with or in response to a sign – it is a practice, a regular use – then we embrace the conclusion that it is not possible to follow a rule 'privately'. The concept of rule-following cannot be unpacked in terms of what is present to a person's mind but presupposes the concept of a technique of use and response:

> And hence also 'obeying a rule' is a practice. And to *think* one is obeying a rule is not to obey a rule. Hence it is not possible to obey a rule 'privately': otherwise thinking one was obeying a rule would be the same thing as obeying it.[32]

THE COMMUNITY INTERPRETATION

The 'community interpretation' of Wittgenstein's consideration of the concept of following a rule construes the notion of practice in Wittgenstein's remark 'And hence also "obeying a rule" is a practice' as a practice of a community; and it represents Wittgenstein as maintaining that what it is for someone to be following a rule cannot be explained without reference to some community the members of which agree in their reactions to examples with the individual in question (i.e., they agree about which cases fall under the rule and which do not). The concept of following a rule – and so the concept of linguistic meaning – can be applied at the individual level only in virtue of the properties of some community: these concepts are inapplicable to a single person considered in isolation.

This community view of the concept of following a rule implies that there must be public criteria for whether there is a rule that an individual is following, and so implies the impossibility of a language that contains names for sensations in which these names are used quite independently of the behaviour and bodily state of the user of the language. So there is an exceedingly simple transition from the conclusion of Wittgenstein's investigation of rule-following – it is not possible to obey a rule 'privately' – to the conclusion of his consideration of words for sensations: it is not possible for there to be a 'private language'.[33]

Now it is not easy to make this community view of the concept of following a rule both plausible and substantial. It is in grave danger of lapsing into triviality if it is explained in such a way that the community whose practice we are to refer an individual's behaviour to does not need to be an actual community but merely a possible community. Christopher Peacocke, who has advanced the community interpretation, writes:

> Nothing in the community view as I have stated it excludes the possibility of a permanently isolated desert-islander rule-follower. The community view can count such a person as a genuine rule-follower if he reacts to new examples in the same way as would members of our own community, or of some other conceivable community.[34]

But if an individual finds it natural to react to examples in a certain way, it must be possible that there should be other people who also find it natural to react in that way. Hence for any individual who reacts to examples in any way whatsoever there is a possible community the members of which react to examples in that same way. And so reference to a community is not placing any substantive constraint upon the concept of following a rule (except perhaps in the case of a 'private language').

The fact is that when Wittgenstein gives the result of his investigation of the concept of following a rule, and he introduces the notion of a practice or, equivalently, a regular use or a custom or an institution or a technique, the contrast he draws is not a contrast between the behaviour of a solitary *individual* (or an individual considered in isolation) and the practice of a community. It is instead a contrast between a solitary *occasion* (which may involve more than one individual[35]) and a practice which pertains to many occasions. Thus in *Philosophical Investigations*:

> Is what we call 'obeying a rule' something that it would be possible for only *one* man to do, and to do only *once* in his life? . . .
> It is not possible that there should have been only one occasion on which someone obeyed a rule. It is not possible that there should have been only one occasion on which a report was made, an order given or understood; and so on. – To obey a rule, to make a report, to give an order, to play a game of chess, are *customs* (uses, institutions).[36]

And in *Remarks on the Foundations of Mathematics*:

> i) we should not call something 'calculating' if we could not make such a prophecy [as that people we judge to obey the rules of multiplication will reach the result 625 when they multiply 25×25] with certainty. This really means: calculating is a technique . . .
> This consensus belongs to the essence of *calculation* . . .
> In a technique of *calculating* prophecies must be possible.
> And that makes the technique of calculating similar to the technique of a *game*, like chess.
> But what about this consensus – doesn't it mean that *one* human being by himself could not calculate? Well, *one* human being could at any rate not calculate just *once* in his life.
> ii) The application of the concept 'following a rule' presupposes a custom. Hence it would be nonsense to say: just once in the history of the world someone followed a rule (or a signpost; played a game, uttered a sentence, or understood one; and so on).
> iii) In order to describe the phenomenon of language, one

41

      must describe a practice, not something that happens once, *no matter of what kind.*

iv) It is possible for me to invent a card-game today, which however never gets played. But it means nothing to say: in the history of mankind just once was a game invented, and that game was never played by anyone . . .

    In the same way it cannot be said either that just once in the history of mankind did someone follow a sign-post. Whereas it can be said that just once in the history of mankind did someone walk parallel with a board . . .

    The words 'language', 'proposition', 'order', 'rule', 'calculation', 'experiment', 'following a rule' relate to a technique, a custom.[37]

This is just what we should expect. Wittgenstein's thesis is that it is the use someone makes of a sign, not the nature of what comes before his mind when he uses it, that determines the meaning of the sign for him. He has argued that having something before one's mind on one or a number of occasions involving a sign is insufficient for one to be following a rule. And he has replaced this inadequate conception with the idea that to be following a rule one must have a mastery of a practice, a technique, a method of use, and this mastery must be manifested in what one does with or in response to a sign. He underlines this point by emphasising that no matter what happens on a particular occasion this is insufficient in itself for someone then to be following a rule. Hence the concept of following a rule must be explained in terms of a practice, not something that happens once.[38]

RATIONALISM AND THE CHAIN OF REASONS

Now when someone understands a sign interpretation may take place. Perhaps it is only when he translates a sign in one language into a sign in a language he is familiar with that he understands the first sign. But translation merely replaces one sign with another. For there to be understanding interpretation must come to an end, and there must be something other than interpretation. Grasping the sense of a sign cannot consist in interpretation:

grasping the sense of a sign is not a state of consciousness and there need be nothing present to the mind other than the sign that is understood. The sign with which interpretation ends – and usually the original sign will not need an interpretation – is not a peculiar kind of sign, or one that is present to the mind in a special way, which precludes (further) interpretation. Rather, the sign with which interpretation comes to an end is 'a psychological, not a logical terminus'.[39] The sign is reacted to without interpretation. And we have now arrived at the heart of Wittgenstein's opposition to rationalism.

Wittgenstein's opposition to a rationalistic account of the understanding and meaningful use of language is apparent in the very first language-game he describes in *Philosophical Investigations*:

'But how does he know where and how he is to look up the word "red" and what he is to do with the word "five"?' – Well, I assume that he *acts* as I have described. Explanations come to an end somewhere.[40]

Wittgenstein emphasises in many places the fact that in training or teaching other people, explanations of what they are to do come to an end somewhere. This is the counterpart of the fact that in my own case the reasons I have for applying or responding to signs in the way I do come to an end. If understanding a sign were a state of consciousness – if it were a matter of what comes before the mind in addition to the sign – then when I apply a sign that I understand I would have present to my mind that which determines whether the sign applies in the present situation. My interpretation of a rule would provide me with a sufficient reason, a logically conclusive reason, a perfect justification, for believing that *this* is what is required by the rule: it would determine what I have to do in order to follow the rule in any particular case.[41] But since an interpretation does not determine meaning it does not determine what I have to do to follow a rule of which it is an interpretation.

It is therefore a mistake to think that I should always be able to answer the question 'How do you know that this is what you ought to do, that this is the right word to use in this case?' no matter how many times the question is asked in response to the

43

replies I give. If this were a reasonable requirement language would not exist. Hence:

> *We need have no reason to follow the rule as we do.* The chain of reasons has an end.[42]

And when my reasons give out I *act*, even though I have no further reasons. The answer that Wittgenstein gives to the question 'How do I know that this colour is "red"?', or 'How do I know that in working out the series +2 I must write "20004, 20006" and not "20004, 20008"?', or to the general question 'How do I know how to follow the rule in the particular case?', is this: I know how I have to follow the rule in the particular case (and so on) in the same sense in which I know what the word 'help' means when I am drowning and shout 'Help!'. This is how I react in this situation; I am in no doubt as to what to do.[43] The way of grasping a rule that is not an interpretation of the rule is therefore this: being such as to act in a certain way in response to the rule 'without appealing to anything else for guidance'.[44]

AGREEMENT IN JUDGEMENTS

A person's understanding of a rule is made manifest in the use he makes of it. How he understands the rule depends upon what he does at a particular point or in a certain situation. If he acts one way, under the impression that *this* is what he is required to do, he will be credited with one understanding of the rule; if he acts otherwise, again under the impression that this is what the rule requires, he will be credited with a different understanding. It follows that if he does not do what we do then he is not following the rule that we are following. And if we cannot see any kind of regularity in what he does – if we cannot learn to proceed as he does – we will not judge that he is following a rule; perhaps we will judge that he is not following any rule.[45]

Now if we are to use language to communicate we must mean the same by the words we use. What does this require? It requires not that we give our words the same interpretation – we do not need to give them any interpretation – but that we should grasp these words in that manner which is not an interpretation, and that our grasp of these words should be the same: we must form the same concepts. And this means that there must be non-collusive agreement in the use of words and in reactions to them, where this agreement is not explained by the fact that each of us has sufficient reason to believe that *this* is what we have to say or do to be true to what our words mean. Only if there is this kind of agreement, which is not ultimately founded in reason, as to whether in doing *this* a rule has been obeyed or transgressed will we be following the same rules in our use of words. In Wittgenstein's words:

> We say that, in order to communicate, people must agree with
> one another about the meanings of words. But the criterion for
> this agreement is not just agreement with reference to
> definitions, e.g., ostensive definitions – but *also* an agreement
> in judgements. It is essential for communication that we agree
> in a large number of judgements. [46]

Wittgenstein's view that if language is to be a means of communication between people there must be agreement in judgements is misrepresented by the community interpretation of Wittgenstein's investigation of the concept of rule-following as the thesis that an individual can be said to mean something by a word only with reference to a community of which he is (in some sense) a member. But up to the point in *Philosophical Investigations* at which he announces his conclusion that there must be agreement in judgements if language is to be a means of communication Wittgenstein has not attempted to show that it is impossible for there to be something properly called language unless communication is possible by means of it. To reach this conclusion he needs to demonstrate the impossibility of a 'private language'. This demonstration takes place in his investigation of the language of sensations. Although it is intimately linked with his consideration of the concept of rule-following, it is not connected with this in the way maintained by the community interpretation. Wittgenstein's investigation of the language of sensations is the topic of the next chapter.

III

SENSATIONS AND
SENSE-IMPRESSIONS

THE MYTH OF THE GIVEN

It is in general true that whatever my judgements or assertions are about there are two possibilities: either they are justified to some degree or they lack any justification. About most kinds of subject-matter I may or I may not lack sufficient reason, or even any good reason at all, for believing what I do. In these cases my judgement can be either well-founded or unfounded: I can possess or lack a justification for it. Furthermore, it can be either true or false. Accordingly, if my judgement is of this kind, I can have good reason for my belief and in fact be informed of the truth of the matter; or I can have good reason for my belief although it is actually false; or I can have no good reason, or insufficient reason, for a false belief; or, finally, what I believe can, fortuitously, be true even though my reasons are insufficient.

But there appears to be one subject-matter about which I always have, and cannot but have, the perfect justification for my judgements or sincere assertions and about which I cannot be mistaken: (the simple properties of) the intrinsic character of my present sensuous experience – my present sensations, sense-impressions, and related phenomena.[1] The reason this subject-matter seems to have such a privileged position arises from its distinctive relationship to the judgements made about it. For most kinds of assertion that I might make, what I say can be insecurely based. Such remarks can rest on illusion or various other forms of error, or can merely lack the evidential basis they require. It may be that I have no evidence for what I sincerely say or it may be that what I say goes beyond what I have evidence for: my evidence entitles me to say only so much, but I am led by the general structure of my beliefs and by my temperament to form a belief that is not merely a representation of my evidence, but instead a construction that is based upon but goes beyond this evidence. And, of necessity, this is hazardous. By going beyond my evidence I may fall into error: my construction may be a misconstruction. But if my remarks are restricted to the intrinsic character of my present 'state of consciousness' they have, it seems, an absolutely sure foundation. My judgements about the intrinsic character of my present sensations and sense-impressions do not go beyond the evidence upon which they are immediately based, and, accordingly, I am always fully entitled to make them. My beliefs are about what is present to my consciousness and the contents of my consciousness are revealed to me if I direct my attention to them. And since I am directly aware of my present state of consciousness, if my beliefs are confined to its current condition they cannot be in error. This privileged position in which I stand to my present sensations is of course mine alone. For other people can never have as good reason for their beliefs about my present sensations as I have for my own beliefs about them. Their beliefs about my present sensations must go beyond the evidence on which their beliefs are based, and so can never be as securely based as my own beliefs.

This conception that our beliefs about our present sensations rest upon an absolutely secure foundation – the myth of 'the given' – is one of the principal objects of Wittgenstein's attack in his consideration of the concept of sensation. It is by reference to his rejection of this conception that his thought can best be understood.

MICROCOSM AND MACROCOSM

Wittgenstein identified a certain play of the imagination that is associated with this conception of the self-ascription of present sensations. It is, he believed, natural to form a picture of the items about which we seem to have such perfect knowledge. This

47

picture is constructed on the model of the material world and our access to this world in perception. So we imagine that for each of us there is a 'world of consciousness',[2] a 'realm of consciousness',[3] in which our sensations occur and into which nobody else can see. Accordingly, there is an 'external world' and a set of 'internal worlds': we live together in the macrocosm, but we each possess a world of our own, our microcosm. The external world is built of one kind of material (matter), whereas an internal world is built of another kind of material (mind).[4] A world of consciousness does not require the existence of matter to sustain it and its contents are not composed of matter. The items in our internal world do not exist inside us in the sense in which physical events take place inside our bodies. For other people can (but usually do not) look into the interiors of our bodies, and the events that occur there are events in the 'external' world and are composed of matter. An 'inner' object is necessarily hidden from everyone but the person in whose mind, in whose inner world, it exists.[5] Whereas I can observe directly the contents of my own mind, other people can at most speculate about these contents on the basis of what they can observe (my body and its environment). My experiences, the objects in my world of consciousness[6] – the objects in my subjective space – are visible only to me. In short: the 'content' of an experience of mine is a 'private object' that I observe within my consciousness and that another can never observe.[7]

This familiar picture, as I have outlined it, is in many ways incomplete.[8] But it is difficult to imagine how it could be finished in such a way as to render it truly attractive. And it is precisely its lack of finish that enables it to exert a malign influence. The most fundamental of its defects is not, however, its incompleteness. For it would be flawed no matter how it was finished. The picture represents us as having perceptual access to the contents of our own world of consciousness, but not to the contents of any other world of consciousness. But if the contents of a world of consciousness are to be essentially private, they must be non-physical items; and whilst this would neatly explain why others cannot observe them, it would render problematic the owner's own access to them, which has been represented as a form of observation. Furthermore, unless this problem can be overcome, a person will lack any awareness of his own private objects and will therefore not be in a position to say anything about them. It is characteristic of Wittgenstein's approach to philosophy that his investigation of the concept of sensation should concentrate in a highly original way on this basic weakness of the picture.

THE PRIVATE OBJECT OF INTERNAL OBSERVATION

The idea of sensations as private objects of internal observation leads, first of all, to the idea that words for sensations must be taught *indirectly*.[9] A person can learn the meaning of words that name or describe the intrinsic character of sensations only if he observes in his own case instances of what these words refer to: his inner sense must show him what a pain is, what an impression of the colour red is, and so on. But we cannot directly observe, on any occasion, that the kind of private object we want someone to use a word as the name of is present to his mind. In consequence, our mode of teaching the meanings of words for sensations is indirect, for we want our pupil to correlate such a word with something we do not observe on any of the occasions in question, but which we hope he will observe within himself on those occasions.

But of course the situation quickly worsens. For if the contents of one person's mind are hidden from the minds of others in the radical way that is implied by the idea of the private object of internal observation, our conception of what we have reason to believe about other people's sensations and their understanding of the words they use to say what these are requires revision of an equally radical kind. This can be shown in the following manner. If we accept the idea of the private object of internal observation, the undeniable fact that the word 'pain' is the name of a certain kind of sensation is transformed into the idea that the word 'pain' is the name of a certain kind of private object. Now consider the two propositions:

(1) For each person who uses the word 'pain' to ascribe pain to himself there is a certain kind of private object, instances of which the person uses the word 'pain' to refer to in his self-ascriptions of pain.
(2) There is a kind of private object such that for each person

49

who uses the word 'pain' to ascribe pain to himself, he uses the word to refer to instances of this kind.

It is clear that (1) does not entail (2): $(x)(\exists y)\ (xRy) \nrightarrow (\exists y)(x)$ (xRy). The natural thought that there is a common understanding of the word 'pain' and that each of us says the same of another person when we ascribe pain to him as we say of ourselves when we self-ascribe pain requires that we should be assured of the truth of (2). But it follows from the conception of the private object of internal observation that we could have no good reason to believe (2). Yet it is equally clear that nothing assures us of the truth of (1).[10] Hence, if we are to say only what we might be in a position to know, our claim should be personal and not plural:

(3) When I ascribe pain to myself I use the word 'pain' to refer to instances of a certain kind of private object.

For the idea of the private object of internal observation is such that all I can do is to speculate fruitlessly about the existence and nature of any private objects other than those that are or have been present within my world of consciousness. And yet it is these private objects that seem all-important in our understanding of the nature of consciousness. Words for sensations appear to stand for various kinds of private objects. But there is no way in which anyone could know that another person uses such words in self-ascription to name the same kinds of private objects as he himself does, and, consequently, the idea that there is a common understanding of words for sensations is groundless.

CRITIQUE OF THE PRIVATE OBJECT: I

Wittgenstein expressed his opposition to the idea that we possess a perfect justification for our belief about our present sensations and the associated picture of sensations as private objects of internal observation in a number of connected remarks:

(i) I do not identify my sensation by criteria.[11] (I just use the same expression.)

(ii) I cannot be said to learn of my present sensations.[12]

(iii) Whereas a true sentence in the third person present that ascribes a sensation to someone transmits information, a true sentence in the first person present is akin to an expression (*Äusserung*) of sensation.[13]

(iv) When I say 'I am in pain' I use the word 'pain' without a justification.[14]

(v) The verbal expression of sensation is not the report of (the result of) any observation.[15]

(vi) A sensation is not an object.[16]

(vii) I do not derive the words in my verbal expression of a sensation from the sensation.[17]

The basic thought that underlies these various formulations is easy to grasp. For someone to identify something by a criterion is for him to identify it by a method, the application of which he can cite in answer to the question 'How do you know it is . . .?' or 'What reason do you have for saying that it is . . .?'.[18] The method provides him with a justification for his identification: he judges that something falls under a certain concept, and there is some other proposition that is his reason for believing what he judges to be true and which he accepts as a result of using some method for determining the truth of the matter.

Now it was Wittgenstein's view that 'I don't know whether I am in pain or not' – 'I know what "pain" means; what I don't know is whether *this*, that I have now, is pain' – is not a significant proposition.[19] Accordingly, someone who understands 'pain' has no means or method that he can use to find out whether he can truly say that he is in pain, the application or findings of which he can cite as his reason for believing what he asserts. For if there were a method that someone who understands 'pain' could use to find out whether it would be true to say 'I am in pain', it would be possible that he should fail to apply this method (hence the possibility of at least ignorance), or that something should go wrong in its application (hence the possibility of error).[20] If he knows that he has not made use of the method, or if he suspects that something might have gone amiss in his use of it, he could be in doubt as to whether he is in pain and it would be significant for him to say 'I don't know whether I am in pain or not'. Since this is not significant, someone who understands 'pain' cannot make use of a method for determining when he can truly utter the sentence 'I am in pain'. He cannot be in the dark as to whether he can truly say that he is in pain and resolve his uncertainty, come to learn what the truth is, by the application of some method of discovery. He does not learn or fail to learn of his sensations: he does not have some means that he can use to acquire information about their intrinsic characters ((ii) above).

The question 'How does a person know when he can truly say that he is in pain?', where this question is asking for the *basis* of the person's assertions, is misplaced if the person knows what the word 'pain' means. His assertions lack any basis. The answer to the question 'How does he know when he can correctly assert that he is in pain?' – where this means 'By reference to what, by the use of which method, does he find out that he is in pain?' – is 'By nothing at all'. He does not identify his sensation by criteria, but on the various occasions when he is in pain he uses, or is willing to use, the same word 'pain' ((i) above).

There is no intermediate step available to someone who understands the word 'pain' – a step such that if he takes it he is then in a position to assert that he is in pain – that would provide him with a reason for his self-ascription of pain and without which he would not know what to say: his apprehension of when he can truly say that he is in pain is unmediated. Without the employment of any method of discovery, he finds himself able sincerely to say 'I am in pain', as he can find himself groaning with pain. In this way his self-ascription of pain is akin to an expression of pain ((iii) above).

Hence it is incorrect to maintain that the reason I have a right to be absolutely certain that I can truly say that I am in pain is that my remark has an absolutely secure basis, or that I have unshakeable evidence, or that I have an overwhelmingly good justification for what I say. My remark rests on nothing at all, in the sense that I have no reason that assures me of the probable or certain truth of my remark. My remark is ungrounded: in the self-ascription of pain I use the word 'pain' without a justification ((iv) above).[21]

It follows that there is no kind of observation of anything, the result of which I report when I sincerely assert that I am in pain.

The verbal expression of a sensation is not based upon observation of oneself ((v) above).

And *if* we conclude from this that a sensation is not the sort of thing that can be observed, and if we say that something is not an 'object' unless it can be observed,[22] we can derive the conclusion that sensations are not objects ((vi) above). This leaves just the last formulation ((vii) above) of Wittgenstein's underlying thought unexplained, and I now turn to this. The point is by now a familiar one.

DERIVING A NAME FROM AN OBJECT

When I form an image and express in words what I have formed an image of, or when I have the experience as of seeing a certain colour and express the character of the experience in words, or when I have a sensation and express in words the nature of the sensation I experience, 'the great difficulty here', Wittgenstein writes, 'is not to represent the matter as if there were something one *couldn't* do. As if there really were an object, from which I derive its description, but I were unable to shew it to anyone'.[23] The thought that underlies his remark is that it is mistaken to construe my expression in words of my present state of consciousness on the model of my description of a material object, by regarding my present state of consciousness as something that I, but only I, can observe (a 'private object'). This misconstruction involves crediting me with a reason for what I say when I express my image, sense-impression or sensation, a reason that justifies what I say, as I can have a reason that justifies my use of the word 'red' in a description of a material object. In this latter case, if I am asked to justify my description, one thing that I can do is to appeal to a colour chart that contains a sample of the colour correlated with the word 'red'. I can point to the sample and say 'This colour is called red and this material object is, as you can see, the colour of the sample'. I see a material object and I say that its colour is red. I could see something else that is agreed to exemplify the word 'red', and I could derive the word that I use to describe the material object from this second thing – this thing that correlates word and sample. Even when I don't in fact derive the word from the colour chart, I could justify my use of the word 'red' in this way by reference to a rule in accordance with which I use the word; just as someone who has been taught the word 'red' by reference to some particular thing that exemplifies the colour could explain why he used the word 'red' in some later case by referring to the sample and the claim that the object matches the sample.[24]

Now – to take the case of the image first – my image of red is not something I observe and of which I have somehow been informed by others that something of this kind is called 'an image of red'. I don't learn that an image of the colour red *looks like this* or is *this sort of thing*.[25] The fact is that I do not use any criterion to determine whether I have an image of the colour red.[26] My verbal expression of my image is criterionless. When I render my image in words I cannot justify what I say by reference to an exemplary image: an image that can be seen to match the present image and that is agreed to be an image of red. The idea that I derive my description of my image from an object that only I can be directly aware of collapses: I could not apply any rules to derive from a private object the right words for my image.[27]

We have already seen that the verbal expression of pain is not the report of an observation (of something only I can directly observe). When I assert that I am in pain I am not describing something I observe 'within' myself. Hence, I cannot be said to *derive* my words from what I observe. I cannot derive my words from my pain, for this is not something I observe. When I am in pain and I say sincerely 'I am in pain', my utterance is not mediated by an observation of something or other from which I could derive the words I utter.[28]

Finally, I cannot derive the word 'red' from my visual sense-impression as of seeing the colour red, but only from something that is red, i.e., from a sample of red. I cannot read off the description from something I observe. I cannot adduce the sense-impression as my justification for my utterance.[29]

Hence, the self-ascription of sensations can be said to be underived ((vii) above).

MEMORY–SAMPLES

Now it might be thought that the role that a sample of the colour red plays in the description of public objects could be played by a *memory-sample* of a private object of a certain kind in the description of private objects: so that if my sense-impression is thought of as a private object I could still derive my description of it from the impression itself: if my pain is thought of as a private object I could derive my description of it from the pain itself by reference to a memory-image of pain, which functions as a sample does; and so on.

But this thought would be mistaken. For if I have forgotten or I am unsure what colour 'red' is the name of, I can look up a chart that correlates the word with a sample of the colour and thereby provide myself with a justification for using or withholding the word 'red' in my description of this public object that confronts me. But if I have forgotten or I am unsure what kind of private object 'S' is the name of – if I cannot remember which kind it is the name of – I could not look up a chart that correlates the word with a sample of the private object kind in order to regain assurance. The most I could do would be to form an image of such a chart. For such a chart correlating samples and words could exist only in my mind – in my memory or imagination – because the samples it contains are samples of kinds of private object. But my forming an image of a chart of this sort could not provide me with a justification for using, or for declining to use, the word 'S' in my description of the private object that is now present to my mind.[30] A memory-image is not a sample that I can see but that others cannot see, and by reference to which I can establish that 'S' is, or is not, the right word to use for this private object. My appeal to a memory-image is not a matter of my looking up to see which sample is correlated with 'S'; it is, rather, my remembering, or my attempting to remember, which sample does go with 'S'. If I am unsure that 'S' is the right word to use for this private object, i.e., I am unsure what 'S' means, an appeal to a memory-image will not enable me to reach firmer ground; for I must remember which sample is correlated with 'S', i.e., what 'S' means, and this is just what I am in doubt about.[31]

It is therefore mistaken to believe that the role that a sample plays in the description of public objects could be played by a memory-sample in the description of private objects. Accordingly, the conclusion holds: I could not apply any rules to derive from a private object the right word for it.

PUBLIC AND PRIVATE LANGUAGES

We have now worked through a number of formulations of Wittgenstein's opposition to the idea of a sensation as a private object of internal observation: an item that cannot be misidentified by the subject in whose consciousness it exists, and which provides the subject with a perfect justification for his beliefs about it. And we have seen that this opposition can be expressed in the thought that a sensation is not an object: my sensations are not the contents of a subjective space, into which only I can see. When I express my sensation in words I do not observe a private object, see it just as it is, and then render it in words. If my sensations were items that I observed with an internal eye, then when I express my sensation in words I would have a reason or justification for what I say, namely, the evidence of my inner sense. But the words I use to express my sensation I use without a justification: I do not identify my sensation by criteria.

But if this is so, what is the right account of the grammar of names of sensations? Immediately prior to his consideration of this question Wittgenstein announces the following conclusion – one he has reached as a result of his examination of the concept of following a rule:

> If language is to be a means of communication there must be agreement not only in definitions but also (queer as this may sound) in judgments.[32]

Now in a language that can be used as a means of communication words for sensations are, Wittgenstein insists, 'tied up with' behaviour, which is the 'natural expression of sensation'. For example, the verbal expression of pain replaces the primitive, non-linguistic behaviour in which pain is manifested.[33] It is in virtue of this fact that our common words for sensations can satisfy the requirement that there should be agreement in people's judgements: we apply these words to each other on the basis of each other's behaviour and we apply them to ourselves in conformity with, although not on the basis of, the behaviour-criteria used to determine their application to another.[34]

It is clear that the reason Wittgenstein follows his announcement of the necessity for agreement in judgements in the use of words in a common language by his investigation of sensation-language is that the temptation to believe in private objects of internal observation renders a common language for sensations problematic by removing the possibility of the required agreement. Either a common sensation-language becomes impossible or our understanding of our common names of sensations splits into two parts, one public and the other essentially private. The inclination to conceive of sensations as private objects has many roots. One that Wittgenstein emphasised is this: we express our sensations in language independently of observation of our body, and not only can we experience a sensation without manifesting it, we can behave as though we are experiencing the sensation when we are not.[35] This encourages the idea that the concept of sensation is logically independent of the concept of behaviour: even if our concepts of the various kinds of sensation we have common words for are somehow tied up with forms of behaviour, there could be names of sensations for which this is not true. Wittgenstein attempts to show that it is not possible to sever the connection between the concept of a kind of sensation and the concept of behaviour by inviting us to consider the idea of a 'private language'. In a private language words for sensations are not tied up with behaviour, for the sensations they stand for do not have natural expressions.[36] In fact, these words are used quite independently of the behaviour and bodily state of the user of the language.[37] Accordingly, they cannot meet the requirement of agreement in judgements: the only basis available to another person for making judgements about the private language user's sensations is irrelevant.

Now there are many connections between, on the one hand, the views Wittgenstein has developed in the *Philosophical Investigations* up to the point at which he begins his examination of how words refer to sensations and, on the other hand, the results of this examination. But I do not believe that it is possible to derive the conclusion of Wittgenstein's 'private language argument' – that a private language for one's sensations is impossible – from the conclusion of his consideration of the notion of following a rule – that 'obeying a rule' is a practice and, hence, that it is not possible to obey a rule 'privately'[38] – in the simple manner advanced by the 'community interpretation' of Wittgenstein's discussion of rule-following. For, as I have argued, the community interpretation of the idea of obeying a rule 'privately' is wide of the mark and its understanding of the idea of a 'practice' is unwarranted.[39] Accordingly, it misrepresents the nature of Wittgenstein's argument and credits it with a conclusion that it has not established. In fact, the user of a private language can embrace the thesis that 'obeying a rule' is a practice. He can agree that it is not what comes before his mind when he writes 'S' down that determines whether there is a rule that he is thereby obeying and what this rule is, but rather his use over time of 'S'. He can say that *if* others could be aware of what he is doing they would see, he hopes, that he is following a rule in his use of 'S' – they would react on each occasion as he does if they were to have what he has; and he can say that if they were to contradict him they would, perhaps, be right: he has made a mistake in his application of the term on some occasion or, more seriously, there is no regularity at all in his use of the term. The point is that others *cannot* be aware of what he does, and so they cannot know whether there is regularity or randomness in his behaviour – for others cannot be aware of the nature of the item (if any) to which he applies 'S' on any occasion. Since others can know only *at which* times he uses 'S' and never *what is true* at these times, they are never in a position to pass judgement on his use of the term.

The connection between Wittgenstein's assertion that it is not possible to obey a rule 'privately' and the conclusion of his private language argument emerges when we focus on the real difficulty that faces the user of a private language. This arises from his intention to introduce a sign 'S' *as a name of a sensation* (in order to be able to record in words the recurrence of the sensation).[40] And the difficulty is obvious. For if 'S' is intended to be the name of a sensation it must have the same grammar as a word for a sensation. Now this grammar has two essential components: that which is characteristic of the third-person use of names of sensations, and that which is characteristic of the first-person use. But in the case of the user of a private language there is no third-person use: nothing provides another with a good basis for using the term 'S' to describe the private language user's condition, and nothing provides the private language user with a good basis for using the term 'S' to describe anybody else's condition. Hence, if 'S' has any claim at all to the title of a name of a sensation, it must be used in the way a name of a sensation is used in the first-person – in particular, in the first-person present. And hence, when the private language user thinks 'I have S' he has no reason for believing that this is so: his self-ascriptions are criterionless: he uses 'S' without a justification: in order for him to know when to write down 'I have S' there is nothing he needs to find out about to underwrite his disposition to do so: his thought 'I have S' is groundless. But not only is this insufficient for 'S' to be granted the status of name of a sensation, it is insufficient for it to be accorded the status of meaningful sign or word.

The conceptual difficulty that faces someone who intends to construct a private language emerges with great clarity when we introduce the notion of a private ostensive definition, the kind of definition that is needed to give sense to names of sensations in a private language. The private language user is someone who speaks, writes down or says to himself the sign 'S' at the same time as he concentrates his attention on a sensation – he gives himself a private ostensive definition of 'S'[41] – and then on certain later occasions writes the sign down again. Now his act of private ostensive definition does not give any content to the idea that it would be *correct* for him to write 'S' down on certain subsequent occasions and *incorrect* for him to write 'S' down on certain other occasions. For the combination of an act of attention to a sensation and the utterance of 'This is called "S"' does not determine the meaning of 'S': any ostensive definition can be variously understood.[42] It is the way in which a sign is used, or is intended to be used, that determines its meaning, and the concentration of a person's attention upon a sensation as he speaks or writes down the sign implies nothing about how the sign is to be used. And the combination of an act of attention to a sensation and the utterance of 'This *sensation* is called "S"' likewise does not determine the meaning of 'S': the intention to use 'S' as the name of a kind of sensation of which *this* is an instance leaves indeterminate the nature of the kind in question.

(Compare pointing to a coloured object and saying that 'C' is to be the name of *this* colour.) Furthermore, the intention to use 'S' as the name of a kind of sensation is coherent only if the intention is to use 'S' in the way in which words for sensations are used.[43] The only difference between the first and second styles of ostensive definition is that the second makes explicit use of the concept of sensation and thus shows what place in grammar is to be assigned to the word: it shows the post at which the sign is to be stationed.[44] Hence, the second style of definition merely makes explicit what is presupposed by the first style, namely that the private language user intends 'S' to be the name of a sensation. But this intention requires the private language user to proceed to use the sign in accordance with the grammar of names of sensations, and this is something that he cannot do. As we have seen, his use of the word cannot be the same as the use of a word that is the name of a sensation. The most that the private language user can do is to use his sign 'S' in accordance with *part* of the grammar of the self-ascriptive use of names of sensations. But this implies that when he thinks 'I have S' or writes 'S' down he uses it without a justification: on each occasion when he writes 'S' down he has no reason to do so that justifies him in doing so.

It would be mistaken to think that an appeal to memory would provide the private language user with a justification for what he proceeds to do. We have already seen that a memory-image does not enable us to derive our word for a sensation from the sensation itself in accordance with a rule. And the private language user's thought 'This is an S' receives no support of any kind from his thought 'This is the same as the one I called "S" previously'; for he must say that 'It is an S' is equivalent to 'It is the same as the one I called "S" previously' – the one thought is not on a different level from the other. Hence, all that his mastery of a private language comes to is the fact that he sometimes, without any particular reason, writes the sign 'S' in his diary.[45] And since his use of 'S' is entirely unconstrained, 'S' is not a sign whose use is rule-governed.

This unfortunate consequence for the private language user's use of 'S', in which the abrogation of the normal language-game with the expression in behaviour is assumed,[46] does not hold for a sensation term in a common language. Although such a word is used in self-ascription without justification, this use is not unconstrained; for it must be used in general conformity with what is taken to be indicative of the occurrence of a sensation of the kind in question – the behaviour that is 'expressive' of the sensation (to put the matter very loosely) – if the user of the word is to be deemed to understand what the term means. And so there are restrictions on the use of the word, even though in self-ascription the word is used without a justification: the groundlessness of self-ascription does not imply that there is no rule that is being followed when the word is used. It is precisely because the self-ascriptive use of a word for a sensation is not viable in isolation that 'an "inner process" stands in need of outward criteria'.[47] For the self-ascription of an 'inner process' will be criterionless; and without outward criteria a sign that supposedly stands for the 'inner process' will not be rule-governed. This is why Wittgenstein insists that 'if I assume the abrogation of the normal language-game with the expression of a sensation, I need a criterion of identity for the sensation'.[48] I need a criterion of identity for the sensation in order to give content to the concept of a sensation of that kind.

The private language user is therefore impaled on the horns of a dilemma: either he intends 'S' to be a sign for something that others can have a conception of, or he does not. But if he does not, he is condemned to silence: there is nothing he can say that will make clear to others what kind of sign 'S' is supposed to be. If, on the other hand, he intends 'S' to be a sign which can be explained to others, either he intends it to be the name of a sensation or he intends it to be some other kind of word. But if he intends 'S' to be the name of a sensation, the most he can do is to use it in self-ascription in the way that a name of a sensation is used, and then his use is not rule-governed and he is not using 'S' as the name of a sensation. And he cannot escape from his predicament by retreating from his intention to use 'S' as the name of a sensation and resting content with a weaker intention to use it as some other kind of word, a name of something or other. For the words he uses to explain the nature of 'S' will be words in a common language and his entitlement to use these words requires him to provide a justification for using them that is acceptable to those who have a mastery of the language – and this is something he cannot do, or can achieve only at the cost of rendering his sign one that is not a word in a private language.[49]

Hence, the private language user's thought that he is using 'S' as a sign lacks any foundation.

The conclusion that the supposed use of 'S' as the name of a sensation in a private language amounts only to writing 'S' down from time to time, on each occasion for no justifying reason, enables us to make clear the connection between the two propositions:

(i) It is not possible to use a word as the name of a sensation in a private language,

and

(ii) It is not possible to obey a rule 'privately'.

For if the aspirant private language user merely writes 'S' down on a number of occasions, on each occasion only for the non-justifying 'reason' that he considers it correct then to use 'S', there is only what is before his mind on the various occasions (the sign 'S') to give substance to the idea that he is obeying a rule in his use of 'S'. But, as Wittgenstein has shown, this is insufficient to give content to the notion of obeying a rule. For, otherwise, no matter what the set of occasions is on which someone uses the sign 'S', he will be following a rule in his use of 'S' throughout the series of occasions. And so if the person thinks he is following a rule in his use of 'S', he will be following a rule; because on each occasion when 'S' seems to him to be the appropriate word for the occasion 'S' will be present to his mind. But:

> to *think* one is obeying a rule is not to obey a rule. Hence it is not possible to obey a rule 'privately': otherwise thinking one was obeying a rule would be the same thing as obeying it.[50]

Accordingly, it is not possible to use a word as the name of a sensation in a private language because it is not possible to obey a rule 'privately'. For the use of 'S' by the aspirant private language user comes to nothing more than the sign's coming before his mind in a certain manner on the various occasions of use; and this involves his proceeding 'privately', but not, thereby, obeying a rule. The bridge between the thesis that 'obeying a rule' is a practice and the thesis that 'obeying a rule' is a practice that *can* be common within a community is the distinctive nature of the self-ascription of sensations. Private ostensive definition cannot determine a normative practice – one in which there is a distinction between a correct and an incorrect use of a word.

CRITIQUE OF THE PRIVATE OBJECT: II

It will be helpful if I now bring together the elements of Wittgenstein's attack on the significance of the conception of private objects of internal awareness and the correlative idea of private ostensive definition, which is required to underwrite the concept of private objects. He attacks along three fronts, which are directed against these three issues: (i) the relevance of references to private objects by words that have a public use, (ii) the relevance of constancy of reference to private objects by an individual, and (iii) the coherence of the idea of kinds of private object (and so the coherence of the idea of constancy of reference).

His treatment of the first issue is encapsulated by his familiar and well-understood 'beetle-in-the-box' analogy.[51] The point is a simple one: if each person uses the word 'beetle' as the name of an object the nature of which he can be aware of only in his own case, *and* the word 'beetle' has a use in the people's language, then in its common use it is not being used as the name of an object. That is to say, even if each individual's first-person use of the word has an unproblematic private reference to a certain kind of object (an object nobody else can know about), this fact is immaterial to the functioning of the word in the public language. Applying the analogy to the language of sensations Wittgenstein draws this conclusion:

> if we construe the grammar of the expression of sensation on
> the model of 'object and designation' the object drops out of
> consideration as irrelevant.[52]

Now let us turn to the other two issues. In *Philosophical Grammar* Wittgenstein introduces an illustration that resembles something that looks like a proposition but is not one, and he remarks that the example is akin to a philosophical mistake. It is a design he was once shown for the construction of a motor roller:

The invention consists of a motor inside a hollow roller. The crankshaft runs through the middle of the roller and is connected at both ends by spokes with the wall of the roller. The cylinder of the petrol-engine is fixed onto the inside of the roller. At first glance this construction looks like a machine. But it is a rigid system and the piston cannot move to and fro in the cylinder. Unwittingly we have deprived it of all possibility of movement.[53]

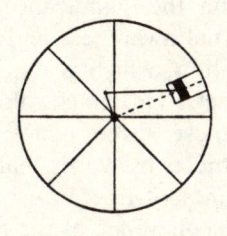

When he refers to this example on a later occasion he relates it to the notion of private ostensive definition:

The example of the motor roller with the motor in the cylinder is actually far better and deeper than I have explained. For when someone shewed me the construction I saw at once that it could not function, since one could roll the drum of the roller from outside even when the 'motor' was not running; but *this* I did not see, that it was a rigid construction and not a machine at all. And here there is a close analogy with the private ostensive definition. For here too there is, so to speak, a direct and an indirect way of gaining insight into the impossibility.[54]

It is not absolutely clear what Wittgenstein had in mind in referring to direct and indirect ways of gaining insight into the impossibility of private ostensive definition. But Wittgenstein's treatment of the relevance of constancy of reference to private objects by an individual and the coherence of the idea of sameness and difference of kinds of private objects can be brought into alignment with the example of the motor roller. The drum corresponds to a person's behaviour in the outer public world, which includes his linguistic behaviour, and in particular his verbal expression of sensation. The motor corresponds to private ostensive definition, the ostensible determinant of the use of sensation words, which are alleged to be used in the manner they are used in the outer world in virtue of an individual's awareness of the occurrence of their private referents in his inner world. The motor's being switched on corresponds to the private ostensive definition's being effective in bringing about the correct use that it supposedly defines; the motor's not being switched on corresponds to the private ostensive definition's having taken place but failing to bring about correct use.

Now consider, firstly, the issue of constancy of reference to private objects by an individual. The source from which correct inner use flows is supposed to be private ostensive definition. But if correct inner use can flow from it, so can incorrect inner use. Corresponding to the possibility of rolling the drum from outside even when the motor is not running is the possibility that correct first-person use of common sensation-words should coexist with incorrect inner use: an individual's verbal expression of his sensations might be in accordance with the behavioural criteria that fix the meaning of the sensation-word in the public language even when he is not correctly recognising the private objects to which his words are intended to have a private reference. So the correct first-person use of names of sensations is not dependent upon the correct identification of events the nature of which is inaccessible to others. From the point of view of the public world, as long as an individual uses a sensation-word in conformity with the criteria that determine its use in the language, it makes no difference if his private references are unreliable – if, not being able to remember correctly the kind of private object he *should* be using the word to refer to inwardly, he called different kinds of private object by the same name:

> 'Imagine a person whose memory could not retain *what* the word "pain" meant – so that he constantly called different things by that name – but nevertheless used the word in a way fitting in with the usual symptoms and presuppositions of pain' – in short he uses it as we all do. Here I should like to say: a wheel that can be turned though nothing else moves with it, is not part of the mechanism.[55]

> Always eliminate the private object for yourself, by supposing that it keeps on altering: you don't notice this, however, because you memory keeps on deceiving you.[56]

If we now combine this point about the irrelevance of

of reference to private objects by an individual with the moral of the 'beetle-in-the-box' analogy, we reach this conclusion: the use of a sensation-word in a public language is independent of any individual's private use of it to name his private objects. The understanding of names of sensations in a shared language is in no way governed by what is true of the world of private objects: it does not matter whether different individuals use such a name privately to designate the same or different private objects or to designate nothing at all, and it does not matter whether any individual's private use is frequently incorrect by the standard supposedly laid down by his private ostensive definition. As far as a public language is concerned, incorrect inner use is just as good as correct inner use, and identity of inner use by individuals no better than difference.

I have previously referred to the picture associated with the conception of the verbal expression of sensation as the perfectly justified report of what is known immediately and incorrigibly: the picture of the two kinds of world, the outer material world and the inner non-material world. Wittgenstein introduces this picture in *The Blue Book* like this:

> At first sight it may appear . . . that here we have two kinds of worlds, worlds built of different materials; a mental world and a physical world. The mental world in fact is liable to be imagined as gaseous, or rather, aethereal. But let me remind you here of the queer role which the gaseous and the aethereal play in philosophy, when we perceive that a substantive is not used as what in general we should call the name of an object, and when therefore we can't help saying to ourselves that it is the name of an aethereal object. I mean, we already know the idea of 'aethereal objects' as a subterfuge, when we are embarrassed about the grammar of certain words, and when all we know is that they are not used as names for material objects. This is a hint as to how the problem of the two materials, *mind* and *matter*, is going to dissolve.[57]

The problem is dissolved by rejecting 'object and name' as the right model for the grammar of the expression of sensation, as Wittgenstein repeatedly makes clear.

When he replies to the charge that he is really a behaviourist in disguise, denying the reality of everything except human behaviour, he explains that the only fiction he has been speaking of is a *grammatical* fiction.[58] This grammatical fiction is the idea of the private object of internal awareness, named by our words for sensations. And this is the force of the apparently mystifying reply he makes to the related accusation that on his view of the matter the difference between pain-behaviour accompanied by pain and pain-behaviour without any pain is that the pain itself is a *nothing*:

> Not at all. It is not a *something*, but not a *nothing* either.[59]

The point is a simple one: the word 'pain' is not the name of a private object of internal awareness (a something), but the word 'pain' has a use (it does not mean nothing). This interpretation of the passage is confirmed by a comparison with the exactly similar point that Wittgenstein makes about the sense or thought expressed by a sentence. The thought cannot be identified with the sentence, since sentences in different languages can express the same thought. But what then is the thought? According to Wittgenstein, we are inclined to make 'it' (the thought or sense) into:

> a shadowy being, one of the many which we create when we wish to give meaning to substantives to which no material objects correspond.[60]
> we say, 'surely the thought is *something*; it is not nothing'; and all one can answer to this is, that the word 'thought' has its *use*, which is of a totally different kind from the use of the word 'sentence'.[61]

Hence Wittgenstein's answer to the remark 'surely the pain is *something*; it is not nothing' is that the word 'pain' has its use, which is of a totally different kind from the use of a name of a kind of material object: the inspection and classification of a perceived object is an inadequate model of a person's awareness of when he can truly say that he is experiencing a certain kind of sensation. His point is again a grammatical one, as the continuation of the passage that rejects the alternatives *something* or *nothing* makes clear:

> The conclusion was only that a nothing would serve just as well as a something about which nothing could be said. We have

only rejected the grammar which tries to force itself on us here.[62]

We can now return to Wittgenstein's motor roller and pick up the remaining issue of the coherence of the idea of sameness and difference of kinds of private objects. Corresponding to the insight that the motor roller is a rigid construction and not a machine at all is the insight that a private ostensive definition is not a definition at all and cannot provide the driving force for the meaningful use of words. The reason why a private ostensive definition is not really a definition is that it cannot establish the meaning of a sign. We have seen that a private ostensive definition fails to give any sense to the idea that the use of the word supposedly being defined would on any future occasion be right or wrong. The ceremony of attention to a private object (the nature of which cannot be captured in our public language) combined with the declaration 'This is called "S"' does not give any sense to 'S': the private object by reference to which 'S' is introduced into the individual's language and in terms of which the meaning of 'S' is supposed to be defined cannot be used as a criterion of correctness of future use. The private object cannot serve as a sample of the sensation kind that 'S' allegedly stands for and no sense can be given to 'This is the *same* sensation again'. The ceremony is therefore idle. Accordingly, there is no sense to the idea that an individual recognises a private object either rightly or wrongly as being of the same kind as one he encountered previously. Hence a private ostensive definition cannot provide the driving force for the meaningful use of words because it fails to give any sense to the idea that an essentially inward use of a word is correct or incorrect. And hence also constancy of reference to private objects is not only irrelevant from the point of view of a public language, but it is an incoherent idea. It is not just that essentially private objects cannot play any role in a public language-game: there cannot be a private language-game with words for essentially private objects. It is this more basic defect in private ostensive definition that I have concentrated on in my exposition of the so-called private language argument.

LACK OF JUSTIFICATION: SELF-ASCRIPTION
AND RULE-FOLLOWING

We have seen that at least these four considerations lie at the heart of Wittgenstein's private language argument:

(i) If language is to be a means of communication there must be agreement in judgements.

(ii) It is the way in which a word is used that determines what meaning it has, not what comes before a person's mind when he uses the word.

(iii) Words for sensations are 'tied up with' behaviour.

(iv) A person does not identify his sensations by criteria.

And the last of these considerations is of crucial importance. Moreover, it provides one link between Wittgenstein's concern with the self-ascription of sensations and his more general concern with the concept of following a rule, and, in particular, with the notion of developing a series of numbers by the application of a formula. For he insists that a formula for performing a mathematical operation does not compel us to make use of it in the particular case as we do, in the sense that our reasons for doing so are not endless. But he believes that we are inclined to look for a justification of a certain kind – a logically conclusive reason – for our applying the formula as we do, and that we are liable to be dismayed when we fail to find such an absolutely firm justification. Now he believes that when we reflect on the self-ascription of present sensations we are liable to experience a similar temptation: we are inclined to look for a justification for our using the word that occurs in our self-ascription when there is no justification.[63] And just as the lack of a perfect justification (as it were) for using a formula in a certain way is actually of no consequence, for in fact people react to instruction and training in similar ways and agree in their judgements as to how the formula is to be applied, despite the fact that the chain of reasons has an end; so the lack of justification for our verbal expression of a present sensation is also of no consequence, for in fact people react to 'training' in the use of names of sensations in similar ways and self-ascribe sensations when others judge that it is true to say of them what they say of themselves. In both cases the requirement for the possession of words in a common language is satisfied and it is satisfied because of our common human nature: we react in similar ways in response to similar exposure to, and training in the use of, language.

SENSATIONS AND CAUSATION

There is, however, one aspect of Wittgenstein's consideration of the grammar of names of sensations that is problematic: the virtual omission of any reference to, and no assessment of the significance of, the crucially important fact that sensations are (or appear to be) events that *cause* the behaviour in which they are 'expressed'. Bodily pain occupies pride of place in Wittgenstein's discussions of the language of sensations and it would seem to follow from the way in which the word 'pain' is used that pains are events suitable to play causal roles.[64] Is this consistent with the rejection of the model of 'object and name' for the verbal expression of sensation?

We can distinguish three causal roles that might be assigned to a pain: (i) it has been caused by something that has happened to or in the subject's body, (ii) it is the cause of the bodily movements in which it is manifested, and (iii) it is the cause of the subject's sincere assertion that he is in pain. Now it would be singularly implausible to deny that the word 'pain' is used in such a way that the concept of pain is the concept of an event that can be caused by what befalls the subject's body. For the language-game played with the word 'pain' is strewn with references to bodily causes of people's pains. But if a pain is an event that can be caused, it can in turn cause other events; and if a person's pain is an event caused by something that happens to his body, then it is available as a source of the person's bodily reactions to the pain. Moreover, it appears to be built into the language-game that the relation between a pain and its behavioural manifestations *is* causal. Hence it would seem that the grammar of the word 'pain' represents a pain as an intermediate event in a causal chain that stretches from the bodily cause to the natural behavioural expressions of the pain. But if this is so, is there a causal relation between a person's pain and his sincere assertion that he is in pain? Is it intrinsic to the concept of the self-ascription of pain that a true self-ascription of pain is caused by what makes it true, the presence of pain in the subject?

Here is a natural line of thought that leads to the conclusion that a pain not only brings about its natural expressions, but also the subject's utterance, the verbal expression of pain (or the internal counterpart of the utterance, the awareness that he is in pain). Someone understands the word 'pain' only if in general his readiness to ascribe pain to himself is in accordance with the behaviour-criteria on the basis of which pain is ascribed to another. There must be a general coincidence of two things: on the one hand, his being able sincerely to utter the sentence 'I am in pain', and on the other hand, his spontaneous inclination to behave in non-linguistic ways that are indicative of his being in pain. Now if this coincidence is not to be a mere coincidence, there must be a causal connection between the phenomena that regularly go together. On the assumption that there is a causal connection between them, its nature seems obvious: an instance of spontaneous pain-behaviour and the self-ascription of the pain responsible for that behaviour have a common cause, and this common cause is the pain the sufferer then feels. So the pain would be a link in the causal chain that runs from the occurrence of damage to the body to the expression of the pain in words or non-linguistic behaviour.[65] I seem to be aware that this is the way things are in my own case: the burning coal caused the pain, which caused me to drop it, and I am in a position to say sincerely that I am in pain only because my thought that I am in pain has also been caused by the pain. But if this is true – if my thought that I am in pain and the behaviour that reveals that I am in pain are caused by my pain – it places a constraint on the correct account of the concept of pain. It is now necessary to state this constraint and examine whether Wittgenstein accepted it.

If the train of thought that leads to the conclusion that a pain brings about its natural expressions, its verbal expressions and its unvoiced recognitions is accepted, a presupposition of the language-game played with the word 'pain' would appear to be that each pain is identical with a physical event that occurs in the body of the subject of pain. Since the causal considerations that apply to pain apply in a similar way to other kinds of sensation, the result would be a general token-token identity between sensations and material events: each sensation is identical with a physical event in the subject's body.[66] If this were so, my sensations would not be 'objects' to me, in as much as I do not observe them; but they would be observable in principle, even by me. A sensation would then be a *something*, but not a something observation of which grounds self-ascription of the sensation. My self-ascription of a sensation would be a form of sensitivity to the presence within me of something – something that has the property of being a sensation of the kind ascribed; but the sensitivity, as far as my uninformed awareness of it reveals it to me, would be brute. That is to say, I would not be conscious of how I know when to say that I am in pain or see the colour red, in the sense that I would not be conscious of the causal mechanism that mediates between the sensation and my consciousness of its presence within me. My criterionless self-ascription of sensations would conform to this pattern: when I self-ascribe 'S' I do not use any method to find out what is happening to me that would provide me with a reason to accept the thought that I am experiencing 'S'; and a physical event, identical with the instance of 'S' in question, causes the thought, its verbal expression if there is one, and the natural expressions of the sensation. Once we abandon the conception of sensations as private objects of internal observation, it is possible to conceive of them as physical events that occur in our bodies and that, although unobserved by us, cause us to have beliefs that are expressible in sentences of the form 'I am in pain', 'I can see the colour red', and so on.

Now it is hard to understand how the inherent suitability of sensations to play a causal role in the production of behaviour could be accommodated by Wittgenstein in any other way than by regarding them as being physical events in people's bodies. For his criticism of the idea of essentially private objects rules out the possibility that sensations might be immaterial sources of the natural expressions and self-ascriptions of sensations. Moreover, the demands made by a token-token identity of sensations and internal physical events are minimal: it is not required that the intrinsic nature of those physical events that are instances of a certain kind of sensation should be the same either across persons or within the same person. But whatever the merits of the suggestion, it is clear, I believe, that Wittgenstein would not have accepted it.[67] The claim that each pain is identical with a physical event in the subject's body derives, basically, from the thought that a pain causes the bodily movements in which it is manifested. But the train of thought I developed was built around the self-ascription of pain. Let us consider this first.

The nature of the capacity to self-ascribe pain – what a correct understanding of this requires, and how we are inclined to misrepresent this to ourselves in false pictures we conjure up when we are bewitched by our language – is one of the leading motives of Wittgenstein's investigation of the philosophical problem of sensation. If he had believed that the capacity to self-ascribe pain must be thought of as being founded in a causal mechanism, whereby a physical event in the body, the occurrence of which is required to make a self-ascription true, produces the inclination to self-ascribe pain, there would surely be some trace of this view in his various investigations of the concept of pain. But it is conspicuous only by its absence. It might be thought that although the postulation of a causal connection between a pain and the subject's self-ascription of that pain is compatible with the criterionless nature of the self-ascription of pain, it is incompatible with Wittgenstein's view that it is senseless to suppose that someone might wonder whether he was in pain or be in error about the matter.[68] This is partly right and partly wrong. Let us suppose that a causal mechanism subserves the self-ascription of pain, so that whenever someone truly self-ascribes pain a physical event in his body, identical with his pain, sets in motion a causal mechanism that produces his self-ascription. Now it must be possible for this mechanism to malfunction. Since it is not of the essence of pain that it should cause a judgement in which it is self-ascribed,[69] one way in which the mechanism might malfunction would be this: although the mechanism is triggered by a pain, it fails to generate a self-ascription of pain. Accordingly, someone who understands 'pain' might properly wonder whether he is in pain, even though he has no inclination to self-ascribe pain. Another way in which the mechanism might malfunction would be this: it generates a verbal expression of the same intrinsic nature as a self-ascription of pain although it has not been set in motion by an appropriate event. But it would be wrong to conclude that someone could therefore

73

be in error in believing himself to be in pain, for this would presuppose that a sincere self-ascription of pain could be identified independently of its cause. If a sincere utterance of 'I am in pain' counts as a self-ascription of pain, manifesting an understanding of the word 'pain', only if it is the effect of the subject's being in pain, the fact that a sincere utterance of the sentence could issue from something other than pain does not open the possibility that someone who understands the word 'pain' might falsely believe he is in pain. So the infallibility of non-inferential self-ascriptions of pain is compatible with the thesis that a true self-ascription of pain must be caused by a physical event in the subject's body, which is identical with the pain he experiences.

Nevertheless, Wittgenstein would have rejected the view that the concept of the self-ascription of pain requires that when a pain is sincerely self-ascribed a physical event in the subject's body, identical with his pain, must cause the self-ascription. It would only be plausible to attempt to pin this view on Wittgenstein if he accepted the necessity of a token-token identity of pains and internal physical events. But his conception of the grammar of words prevented him from acknowledging the necessity for such an identity: the language-game played with the word 'pain' seemed to him to place no requirements on what happens inside people's bodies, and, in particular, it does not demand that each pain is identical with a physical event in the body of the person who experiences the pain. It is because of his commitment to the autonomy of language-games that his consideration of the concept of pain emphasises the manifest causes of pain and the manifestation of pain in primitive natural expressions or more sophisticated forms of behaviour, such as the verbal expressions of pain that replace the non-linguistic expressions of pain.

When Wittgenstein, in his discussion of 'reading', maintains that the concept is 'quite independent of that of a mental or other mechanism',[70] he appears to be embracing a certain conceptual thesis. This thesis claims that if the criteria for the application of 'W' to something can be known to obtain without finding out that a certain proposition is true of that thing, the fact that 'W' applies to something does not require that that proposition should be true of that thing: the concept signified by 'W' is quite independent of the proposition in question. Since the criteria for the application of 'pain' to someone, and the criteria for someone to possess the capacity to ascribe pain to himself, can be known to obtain without finding out that a physical event occurs in the person's body that causes the behavioural manifestations of the pain and the person's readiness to self-ascribe pain, if we were to accept this thesis we would believe that neither the concept of pain nor the concept of the self-ascription of pain imposes the requirement that when someone experiences pain a physical event must occur in his body and cause whatever issues from his pain. Consequently, Wittgenstein's adoption of the conception of language-games articulated by this thesis would be a sufficient explanation of the fact that he does not insist that the occurrence of each pain requires a corresponding or identical physical event in the sufferer's body. It would also account for his not requiring that the explanation of a person's being able to acquire the capacity to self-ascribe pain – a capacity that someone has only if there is a general coincidence of his inclination to behave in ways that are indicative of his being in pain with his readiness to judge that he is in pain – must reside in the fact that when the person is in pain a physical event that causes the non-verbal behaviour that issues from the pain also causes the person's judgement that he is in pain. And it would explain the flavour of behaviourism that is detectible in his examination of the concept of pain and the other concepts of kinds of sensation, despite his attempts to distance himself from behaviourism. For his rejection of the private object (immaterial event) and his refusal to acknowledge the necessity for an internal physical event to bring about the effects of a sensation would preclude him from doing justice to the causality that is an integral element of our understanding of the concept of sensation.

The consequence of trying to steer a middle course between materialism and immaterialism in an account of the concept of sensation is that the idea of a sensation as a cause of its manifestations has to be jettisoned and all the weight has to be taken by the notion of behaviour (both verbal and non-verbal): behaviour expressive of sensation might issue from the chaos that Wittgenstein believed could conceivably lie at the heart of our mental mechanism.[71] The real force of the abandonment of the model of 'object and name' for the verbal expression of sensation becomes apparent only when we understand its true scope: it is not restricted to the rejection of the private object of internal observation, but includes the renunciation of sensations as occurrences with causal powers. But with this wider scope it becomes a revisionist account of the language-game played with names of sensations.

IV

SEEING ASPECTS

NOTICING AN ASPECT AND THE
EXPERIENCE OF MEANING

When we are looking at an object we sometimes see that it has
not changed while we have been looking at it and yet the way in
which we see it has changed: we see it differently, although we
see that it is no different from how it was. For example, we might
pass from seeing a puzzle-picture as mere lines to seeing it as
containing a depiction of a face, from seeing **Figure 1** as a plane
figure consisting of a square and two rhombuses to seeing it as a
picture of a cube, from seeing the ambiguous duck-rabbit **Figure
2** as a duck-picture to seeing it as a rabbit-picture, from merely

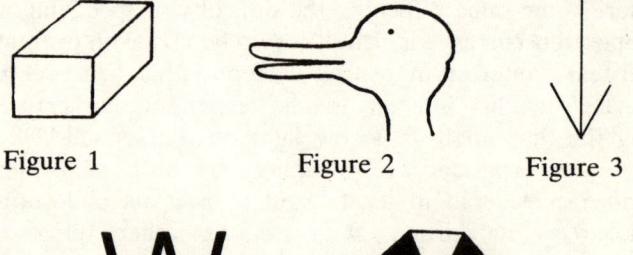

Figure 1   Figure 2   Figure 3

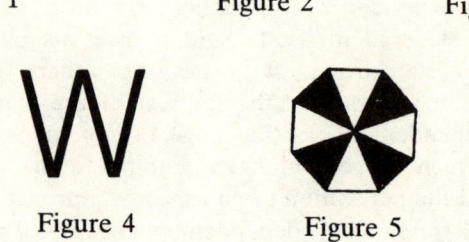

Figure 4   Figure 5

seeing two faces to seeing a likeness between the two, from seeing these four dots . . . . as two pairs of dots side by side to seeing them as two interlocking pairs or as one pair inside the other, from seeing **Figure 3** as a sign in the form of an arrow, pointing in a certain direction, to seeing it as depicting a bird's foot, from seeing **Figure 4** as a capital W to seeing it as a capital M upside down, from seeing the 'double cross' **Figure 5** as a white cross on a black ground to seeing it as a black cross on a white ground.[1] In each case we can be said to notice an *aspect* of what we are looking at.[2] What is it to notice an aspect? When we undergo that kind of change in our way of seeing something that constitutes noticing an aspect of what we are seeing, what happens? What does this change consist in? What constitutes the change from seeing the item one way to seeing it the other way?

Wittgenstein returned to the topic of noticing an aspect time and time again in his later writings on the philosophy of psychology. He was of course concerned not with the causes of the experience but with the concept of it. But why was it so significant for him? One reason for his interest in the concept of seeing an aspect was undoubtedly its close relationship with the idea of experiencing the meaning of a word,[3] as when we utter an ambiguous word by itself, first with one meaning, then with another, or when we utter a word a number of times in a row and 'it loses its meaning, as it were, and becomes a mere sound'.[4] There is a common temptation in the two cases: the temptation to postulate a specific occurrence that constitutes the phenomenon (the perception of the aspect, the experience of meaning). And there is the same difficulty: the difficulty of specifying what this supposed occurrence is. But it would be mistaken to think of Wittgenstein's interest in aspect perception as being entirely derivative from his interest in the experience of meaning, studying the first solely to throw light on the second. On the contrary, the experience of meaning has little philosophical significance considered in itself,[5] and it owes its philosophical importance to its kinship with, among other things, the perception of an aspect. For the interest of the experience of meaning is dependent upon 'the range of similar psychological phenomena which in general have nothing to do with word-meaning',[6] and the perception of an aspect is a principal member of this related class. The independent philosophical importance of the concept of noticing an aspect is due to its location at a crucial point in our concept of the mind – a point from which lines radiate in all directions across the field of psychological phenomena. And the concept of aspect perception provided Wittgenstein with one of the best illustrations of what he took to be a pervasive and misguided reductionist tendency in the philosophy of psychology: the inclination to assimilate elements of the mind to a small set of favoured but inadequate paradigms, as in the case of the empiricist bias towards sense-impressions or the rationalist bias towards varieties of thought.

DIFFERENT KINDS OF ASPECT

But the image of a single point at which the sensory meets the intellectual is not entirely accurate. For there are significantly different kinds of aspect,[7] in which the sensory is joined with the intellectual in different ways and in different proportions. There are also various ways in which we might be seeing an object immediately prior to our noticing an aspect of it. Hence, the kind of change in our way of seeing something in which noticing an aspect consists is not defined by the transition from one particular kind of state to another particular kind of state, but is variously realised: there are many kinds of state from which we can change and there are many kinds of state in which we can find ourselves after the change. For example, we can pass from:

  (i) seeing something which is meaningless to us to seeing the item pictorially,

 (ii) seeing something as a non-pictorial sign to seeing it as a picture (or *vice versa*),

(iii) seeing something as a picture of one kind of thing to seeing it as a picture of another kind of thing,

 (iv) seeing one part of an area as figure and the other as ground to seeing the second part as figure and the first as ground,

  (v) seeing something without seeing a likeness between it and another object to seeing a likeness between the two,

 (vi) seeing something as if it were meant to be one linguistic sign to seeing it as if it were meant to be another linguistic sign,

(vii) seeing a collection of items as grouped one way to seeing the collection as grouped another way.

So the question 'What does noticing an aspect consist in?' dissolves into a number of different questions. For *what*, if anything, ceases and *what*, if anything, takes its place or begins, is not constant throughout the variety of cases in which an aspect is noticed. And this is true even though there is something which, for all cases, is constant through the change in how we see the object. I shall later explain what this constant element is.

Now it will be possible to elucidate the nature of the change in the manner in which we see something when we notice an aspect of it if it is possible to analyse both of the kinds of seeing involved: the seeing that occurs before and the seeing that occurs after the aspect is noticed. Consider the ambiguous duck-rabbit figure and what happens when we pass from seeing it as a duck-picture to seeing it as a rabbit-picture. The states between which we pass are both cases of pictorial perception: in each case we see the figure as a picture. Accordingly, if pictorial perception involves seeing one thing *in* another, in the sense which Richard Wollheim has given to this notion,[8] the change involves moving from seeing one thing *in* the figure to seeing a different, and incompatible, thing *in* it – from seeing a duck *in* the figure to seeing a rabbit *in* it. If, on the other hand, pictorial perception involves seeing something as a symbol that belongs to a scheme that is syntactically and semantically dense and also relatively replete, as Nelson Goodman believes,[9] the change involves moving from seeing the figure as one such symbol to seeing it as another symbol of that sort – from seeing it as a pictorial symbol of a duck to seeing it as a pictorial symbol of a rabbit. If, finally, pictorial perception involves experiencing the region of the visual field in which the figure is presented as being similar in shape to the region of the visual field in which the object depicted would be presented if it were seen from the point of view from which the object has been depicted, as Christopher Peacocke has argued,[10] the change involves moving from seeing the figure and experiencing its presentation in the visual field as being similar in shape to the presentation of one kind of thing to experiencing its presentation as being similar in shape to the presentation of another kind of thing – from experiencing it as being similarly shaped to a duck-presentation to being similarly shaped to a rabbit-presentation. But whatever account of pictorial perception is favoured, analyses of different types of seeing will be needed to elucidate other cases in which an aspect is noticed. Perhaps figure-ground experience can be understood as pictorial perception in which the whole is experienced as a picture in which the area experienced as figure is depicted as being in front of the area experienced as ground[11] – in which case a switch of figure and ground would be merely a specific form of the transition between one pictorial perception and another. But even if this should be so,[12] there are many uncontroversial instances of aspect perception which cannot be reduced to pictorial perception – as when we notice the likeness between two faces.

Now Wittgenstein did not offer any account of pictorial perception. And although he distinguished different kinds of aspect he did not distinguish them by specifying different types of object of sight and defining or analysing the various forms of seeing that are integral to their perception. He did something similar, however. He distinguished different kinds of aspect by reference to the different kinds of description used to report the aspect.[13] But rather than attempting to define or analyse the different kinds of seeing that are correlative with the different kinds of description – the kinds of seeing that are involved when something is seen as falling under the various descriptions – he chose to indicate the differences between the various kinds of seeing in a different manner. The following list of features that Wittgenstein draws attention to as differentiating one kind of aspect from another gives a fair impression of his procedure:

(i) That they [i.e., aspects] are very different from one another is clear: the dimension of depth, for example, sometimes comes into their description, and sometimes not; sometimes the aspect is a particular "grouping"; but when one sees lines as a face, one hasn't taken them together merely visually to form a group . . . .[14]

(ii) I should like to say: there are aspects which are *mainly* determined by thoughts and associations, and others that are 'purely optical', and these make their appearance and alter automatically, almost like after-images'.[15] For example, the principal aspects of the double cross could be said to be 'purely optical' aspects, whereas other ways in which the figure can be seen (e.g., the white cross as the four corners of a piece of paper folded towards the middle) could be said to be 'conceptual' aspects.[16] Sometimes the conceptual is dominant in an aspect. That is to say: Sometimes the experience of an aspect can be expressed only through a conceptual explanation. And this explanation can take many different forms.[17]

(iii) Sometimes *imagination* is required to perceive an aspect (to see a triangular figure as half a parallelogram, or a bare triangular figure as the picture of an object that has fallen over, for example), sometimes not (to see the principal aspects of the double cross, for example).[18] 'The latter seem to be of a more fundamental nature than the former'.[19]

(iv) We can see the duck and rabbit aspects of the duck-rabbit figure only if we are familiar with the appearance of these animals. No analogous condition holds for the principal aspects of the double cross.[20]

(v) When we give expression to our perception of the principal aspects of the double cross we can point to a part of the double cross, but the duck and rabbit aspects cannot be described in an analogous way – here we point to something *not* contained in the figure.[21]

(vi) The principal aspects of the double cross are not essentially three-dimensional: a black cross on a white ground is not essentially a black cross lying on or in front of a white surface, but a black cross surrounded by white. These aspects are not connected with the possibility of *illusion* in the same way as are the three-dimensional aspects of the drawing of a cube or step.[22]

I have said that Wittgenstein did not present any analysis of pictorial perception. And there is a reason for this omission, over and above Wittgenstein's scepticism about the possibilities of reductive definition or conceptual analysis. For his primary concern in the case of every kind of aspect perception, and not only with that kind that involves pictorial perception, was not to clarify the concepts of the kinds of seeing that lie on either side of the dawning of the aspect, but to combat various misconceptions that the phenomenon of noticing an aspect is liable to generate.

The principal form of misconstruction that is likely to result from puzzlement about what noticing an aspect, in any of its manifold realisations, consists in is an inclination to misdescribe it in such a fashion that it is assimilated to some inappropriate model.

ASPECTS OF ORGANIZATION

'One *kind* of aspect', Wittgenstein wrote, 'might be called "aspects of organization" '.[23] When an aspect of this kind is noticed parts of the item seem to 'go together' which before did not.[24] The type of misunderstanding that Wittgenstein wished to correct in the case of this kind of aspect is an illustration of the principal form of misconstruction to which thought about noticing an aspect is vulnerable in general, and it is therefore a good place from which to begin. In general, noticing an aspect can be likened either to a sensory or to an intellectual change. Wittgenstein's target in his remarks about aspects of organization is the view that the perception of such an aspect involves a sensory, rather than an intellectual, change.

Wittgenstein's use of the term 'organization' in speaking of these aspects is a reference to one of the leading ideas of Gestalt psychology.[25] Wolfgang Köhler expressed this conception, in the case of vision, like this:

> In most visual fields the contents of particular areas 'belong together' as circumscribed units from which their surroundings are excluded.[26]

And he held that this 'organization' of the visual field is a *'sensory fact'* – a sensory fact of an elementary kind. These circumscribed units of the visual field, these visual *Gestalten*, are often continuous. But they can also be discontinuous, and they then consist of discrete entities that unite to form a group – as in the case of the stars that we perceive as forming constellations, or this set of six patches:

which is not seen as merely six patches, nor as three groups of two patches, but as two groups of three patches. The claim that organization of the visual field is a sensory fact likens organization to colour – for colour is also a sensory fact; and it insists that organization resembles colour in being an original feature of the visual field, not something that is imported into visual experience by learning: the explanation of sensory organization in general, and of the organized appearance of the visual field in particular, is not to be found in some process of learning by means of which organization is introduced into the sensory field. It follows from this conception of organization as a sensory (rather than an intellectual) fact that a change of the organization of the visual field is a 'real transformation of sensory facts'.

Now in aspect perception there is a change in the person who notices an aspect: he sees the object in a different way. In the case of those aspects that might be called 'aspects of organization', what is seen as belonging together in the material object of sight after the change of aspect is not seen as belonging together before the change[27] – as when someone suddenly sees the solution of a puzzle-picture.[28] The change of aspect would therefore appear to consist in a change in the organization of the person's visual impression. For he sees the same material object in different ways before and after the change. Yet he does not experience a change in what he sees with respect to apparent colour or shape. Hence the change in him – the change in his manner of perception – must be a change in something other than the shape or colour experienced. Accordingly, if the change in his manner of perception is construed as a change in the intrinsic character of his visual impression, a further feature of a visual impression is required, a change in which constitutes the experience of a change of aspect. And this extra feature is 'the organization of the visual impression': a visual impression is organised in a certain way when and only when certain elements in the object are seen as belonging together in a certain manner, that is to say, when a certain aspect is noticed.

But if we take the term 'organization' seriously, and ask what exactly it means to speak of the organization of a visual impression, we find that this idea is unhelpful.[29] For it suggests that what is in question is a feature of the manner in which the spatial/coloured elements of a figure, for example, look to be related to one another – as when, if I see a row of equidistant points as a row of pairs of points whose inner distance is smaller than the outer distance, I can be said to see the row as organized in that way.[30] Now when I look at a row of points it might look to me to be a row of equidistant points or it might look to me to be a row of pairs of points whose inner distance is smaller than the outer distance: in each case I see the row as organized in a certain manner. However, if I see a row of points which looks to me to be a row of equidistant points, and I then see the row as a row of pairs of points whose inner distance is smaller than the outer distance, I do not experience the *illusion* of seeing a row of points which looks to be organized in this way. And in general when I experience an aspect – an aspect of the kind that might be called an 'aspect of organization' – the spatial/coloured elements of the object I am looking at are not misrepresented in my experience as being different from what they were, so that the organization of the object has apparently altered. Hence, an aspect of organization is not the apparent organization of the object.

Perhaps it will be helpful to put the argument again, but somewhat differently. When there is a change in the so-called 'organizational' aspect of a two-dimensional figure, no part of the visual field must seem to change. This is what underlies the thought that the visual impression does *not* change when a change of aspect occurs. The thought that there *is* a change in some *visual* respect requires the postulation of a further visual feature – a feature other than colour or shape. But if organization of the visual field is put forward as the additional visual feature, and a change of aspect is said to involve a change in the organization of the visual impression, then the concept of organization is being used differently from how it is when, for example, the organization of a company is said to change. For in this latter case *how it is* if the organization changes can be described.[31] But a change in the so-called 'organization' of the visual impression is not mirrored by any apparent change in what is being looked at. Hence, it is unilluminating to characterise the supposed extra visual feature as the 'organization' of the visual impression. Furthermore, the claim that there is a third feature of a visual impression, as directly or immediately visual as colour or shape, is not only unilluminating, but obfuscating. It obscures the subject because the insistence that a change of aspect consists in the change of a feature comparable to shape or colour is designed to blind us to characteristics which a change of aspect shares with thought, rather than with what is specific to vision – coloured shapes.[32]

Wittgenstein asserts that if we yield to the temptation to credit a visual impression with the feature of organization – a feature that is comparable to colour in being sensory, rather than intellectual – then we are thinking of a visual impression as an inner object or materialization, the organization of which changes when a change of aspect takes place:

> If you put the 'organization' of a visual impression on a level with colours and shapes, you are proceeding from the idea of the visual impression as an inner object. Of course this makes this object into a chimera; a queerly shifting construction. For the similarity to a picture is now impaired.[33]

> The aspect *seems* to belong to the structure of the inner materialization.[34]

> If the aspect is a kind of organization and if the organization can be compared to the characteristics of shape and colour, then the change of aspect is like a change of apparent colour.[35]

The reasoning that underlies Wittgenstein's claim that the assimilation of the 'organization' of a visual impression to colour and shape is based on the misconstruction of a visual impression as an inner object is clear. Our visual impression represents what we are looking at (Wittgenstein is here considering a puzzle-picture) as being coloured and shaped a certain way: the colour and shape are ostensibly perceived features. If 'organization' is on a par with colour and shape, it also is something ostensibly perceived. But the material object (the puzzle-picture) does not need to appear to change in any respect when the aspect changes. Hence, 'organization' must be a property of something else that is perceived. And this can only be the inner object – the visual impression itself.[36]

SENSATIONAL AND REPRESENTATIONAL
PROPERTIES OF VISUAL EXPERIENCE

Perhaps the issue that Wittgenstein returns to most persistently in his consideration of noticing an aspect is whether noticing an aspect is *seeing* or *interpreting*. When we change from seeing something one way to seeing it another way and thereby notice an aspect of it, do we really see differently or do we merely interpret what we see differently? Does our visual experience change – do we have two intrinsically different visual experiences – or does our visual experience remain constant and the interpretation that we place upon what we see, whose appearance is unchanged, alter? It is precisely the issue of what is included in the intrinsic nature of a visual experience, and what is the criterion for the possession by a visual experience of a certain intrinsic nature, that lies at the heart of, and provides the motivation for, Wittgenstein's examination of noticing an aspect.

Before I consider Wittgenstein's treatment of this question, I believe it will be helpful to examine a recent account of visual experience which has been used to elucidate what happens when the aspect under which something is seen suddenly alters. Although I will argue that this elucidation fails to clarify Wittgenstein's concept *noticing an aspect*, it is useful in focusing attention upon the kind of phenomenon Wittgenstein had in mind and in identifying the difficulty this phenomenon presents.

In *Sense and Content*,[37] Christopher Peacocke draws a distinction between two kinds of intrinsic properties of visual experience: representational and sensational properties. He argues that every visual experience has sensational properties. And he suggests that in all the standard cases of a switch of aspect what happens is that the sensational properties of the experience remain constant, whilst at least some representational property changes. Moreover, the constancy of the sensational properties is supposed to capture the content of Wittgenstein's point that when I notice an aspect I *see* that the object I am looking at has not changed (although I see it differently). I believe that this misrepresents Wittgenstein's thought about seeing an aspect and I will now attempt to show why this is so.

Normally a visual experience represents the environment of the

87

perceiver as being a certain way. The *representational content* of a visual experience is the way the experience represents the world as being. It is given by a proposition and is therefore assessable as true or false. And it is intrinsic to the experience itself: an experience with a different representational content is phenomenologically different. The *representational properties* of a visual experience are those of its properties that it has in virtue of its representational content. The *sensational properties* of a visual experience as those of its properties that it has in virtue of some aspect – other than its representational content – of what it is like to have the experience. The *intrinsic properties* of a visual experience are those properties of it that help to specify what it is like to have the experience: the totality of intrinsic properties fully specifies what it is like to have the experience. Accordingly, the representational and the sensational properties are both intrinsic properties of the experience. It is Peacocke's main claim in chapter 1 of *Sense and Content* that every visual experience possesses sensational properties: each visual experience has intrinsic properties which are not captured by representational content. I accept this claim but reject the suggestion that aspect switches – aspect switches in the sense in which they were the object of Wittgenstein's investigation – are to be understood as alterations in the representational content of an experience whose sensational properties remain the same.

Peacocke asks us to consider this example:

a wire framework in the shape of a cube is viewed with one eye and is seen first with one of its faces in front, the face parallel to this face being seen as behind it, and is then suddenly seen, without any change in the cube or alteration of its position, with that former face now behind the other.

The representational contents of the two experiences are *different*: the wires that form one face of the cube are represented by one of the experiences as being nearer than the wires that form the other face, but as being further away by the other experience. The sense in which the two experiences are nevertheless experiences of the same type is that their sensational properties are the *same*. It is important to realise that the variable component of the representational content of the experiences is not something that accrues to an experience solely in virtue of the perceiver's possession of a concept under which he brings the object seen – as when, in looking at a flower that I can see perfectly clearly, but whose name I cannot recall, I suddenly remember the name and thereby see the flower as, say, a narcissus. The change in the representational content of the experiences of the cubical wire framework is not merely a matter of different concepts informing an unchanging representational core.

Now I propose to accept this account as explicating the sense in which the experience is unchanged when first one, and then the other, face is seen as being the nearer of the two. Does it help us with the cases that were the object of Wittgenstein's investigation? The answer is, No. For Wittgenstein would not have counted this kind of case as one in which an aspect is noticed,[38] and the cases he considers require a different treatment. The type of change in the representational content of a visual experience that takes place in the example of seeing the cubical wire framework differently – a change in the represented distances of parts of what is seen – is absent from the cases that were of special interest to Wittgenstein; and an example of suddenly seeing something differently that consists only of this type of change in the representational content of the experience thereby fails to be an instance of what he had in mind in his examination of aspect perception. The reason he would have excluded the alteration in the perception of the cubical wire framework from the field of aspect perception is precisely that the difference between the first and second experience consists in one face *looking to be*, rightly or wrongly, the nearer of the two faces and then *looking to be*, rightly or wrongly, the further. In the kinds of case that interested Wittgenstein, and to which he restricted the concept *noticing an aspect*, the appearance of the item seen does not change with respect to colour, two- or three-dimensional shape, distance or the distances of any of its parts from the perceiver.[39] It is because the appearance of the item does not change in any of these ways that the transition from seeing it one way to seeing it another way is puzzling. For it is problematic whether the transition from one experience to the other can properly be said to involve a change *in the experience itself*, and so exemplify a difference in *seeing* rather than a difference merely in *interpretation*. How can a change in the intrinsic nature of the experience be accommodated, if there is no change in the appearance of what is seen in any of these respects?

SEEING AND INTERPRETATION

I now return to Wittgenstein's treatment of the question whether noticing an aspect is a matter of a change in our visual experience or a change in our interpretation of what we see – an interpretation founded upon a constant visual experience.

It is essential to clarify what Wittgenstein means here by 'interpretation'. He explains the concept in the following way. In the first place, what we are concerned with is an *act* of interpreting:

> You see it conformably, not to an interpretation, but to an act of interpreting.[40]

Interpreting is something we do: it is an action.[41] Secondly, what we do when we interpret is 'we make a conjecture, we express a hypothesis, which may subsequently turn out false'.[42] For example, the following illustration might occur at different places in a book:

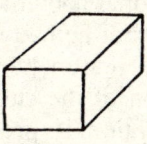

and might be intended one time as a picture of a glass cube, another as a picture of a wire frame, another as a picture of a lidless open box, another as a picture of three boards forming a solid angle.[43] When we interpret the illustration, rightly or wrongly, we take it that this is what it is meant to be: we understand it as intended to be a picture of a glass cube, a wire frame, a lidless open box, or three boards forming a solid angle. In this case, the kind of conjecture or hypothesis involved in interpreting something we see is a conjecture as to *what the item is meant to be*.

Now in fact this notion of interpretation is not especially suitable for Wittgenstein's purposes. For it does not cover the full range of cases of seeing an aspect that he considers. It is not well suited to the example Wittgenstein uses in *Philosophical*

Investigations to introduce the concept *noticing an aspect*: noticing a likeness between two faces. And it is not appropriate to Wittgenstein's double cross, or many other examples, unless what is in question – as it need not be – is what the figure is intended to be. The intention of the designer of the figure may be immaterial to us when we notice an aspect of it. Accordingly, the question whether seeing an aspect is really seeing or really interpreting is not as all-embracing as the question whether it is seeing or thinking. For, given Wittgenstein's conception of interpretation, not all thinking is interpreting, even though 'to interpret is to think',[44] 'interpreting is a kind of thinking'.[45] Wittgenstein writes:

> 'Is it thinking? Is it seeing?' – Doesn't this really amount to 'Is it *interpreting*? Is it seeing?'.[46]

But the question should not be understood in this way if it is to have the generality it requires – if it is to pose the crucial question that can be raised about any case of aspect perception. The notion of interpretation that Wittgenstein expounds is therefore too strong to do the work he intends it for. A better understanding of the idea of interpretation would not restrict interpreting to the making of a conjecture but would allow in cases in which we are only entertaining a supposition, merely imagining or making-believe that a figure is intended a certain way – as in Wittgenstein's case of the arbitrary cipher, which can be seen in various aspects according to the fiction we surround it with.[47] And even this more liberal understanding of interpretation would not have the generality of the notion of thought or conception. However, for ease of exposition I will continue to formulate the issue in terms of the idea of interpretation, and I will later indicate the point at which this notion of interpretation weakens Wittgenstein's argument.

Let us return to the illustration that can be interpreted in so many different ways. When we see this figure and interpret it in one way or another, we can not only see it and interpret it but see it *as* we interpret it. The question is, How are seeing and interpreting connected when we see it as we interpret it? And the 'question whether what is involved is a seeing or an act of interpretation arises because an interpretation becomes an expression of experience'.[48] We describe our experience when we notice an aspect in terms of the interpretation in accordance with which we see the object: 'First I saw it as a [picture of a] glass cube, then I saw it as a [picture of a] wire frame'.

DIRECT AND INDIRECT DESCRIPTIONS
OF ASPECT PERCEPTION

But although we describe the experience in terms of an interpretation, does the intrinsic nature of the experience have an essence that is independent of the nature of the interpretation? Is it in principle possible to specify the intrinsic nature of the experience that we have when we see something in accordance with a certain interpretation independently of that interpretation? Can the nature of the interpretation be separated from the nature of the experience? Or is the interpretation partly constitutive of the experience?

Wittgenstein deals with this issue by considering the temptation to think that seeing in accordance with an interpretation must have an essence, of which a description in the words of the interpretation is only an *indirect* description.[49] The idea that lies behind this temptation is this: there are various interpretations, A,B,C . . . that can be put upon a certain figure; there are various ways, A',B',C' . . . of seeing the figure, or, in other words, various kinds of intrinsically different visual experience, A',B',C' . . . ; and we use interpretation A as a description of A', B as a description of B', C as a description of C', and so on, *because* A' favours interpretation A, B' favours B, C' favours C, and so on. The interpretation we use as a description of a visual experience, a way of seeing, is the one to which the experience is favourable, and we describe the experience in terms of that interpretation because that is the interpretation it favours.[50] But these descriptions are only indirect descriptions of the natures of the experiences they represent. For each of these experiences has a character of its own, and this character merely favours a particular interpretation: the character of the experience does not require the interpretation to be used if its nature is to be specified fully.

Even if we leave on one side the question why experience A' should favour the figure's being given interpretation A, it is clear that we should not succumb to this temptation. For A' – an experience the intrinsic nature of which does not need to be described in terms of interpretation A, and whose nature differs from the intrinsic nature of B',C', and so on – is a myth. It is a myth because there is no more direct linguistic expression of the experience we have when we see the figure in accordance with interpretation A than 'I am seeing it as an A'. The inclination to use the verbal expression is a characteristic *utterance* (Äusserung) of the experience – not a *symptom*.[51] The use of the words that give the interpretation is the *primary* expression of the experience: it is not an indirect description.[52] For if it were only an indirect description – as 'the colour of blood' is an indirect description of a colour – it should be possible to describe the experience directly.[53] But this is not possible. The description using the terms of the interpretation is essential to the description of the experience of seeing in accordance with that interpretation. The experience signified by the words 'seeing the figure F as a mirror-F' requires the concept of a mirror-F to individuate it. The thought of the special *relationship* which the word 'mirror-F' designates is integral to the experience of seeing the figure as a mirror-F.[54] Similarly, when we see a triangular figure as half a parallelogram[55] there is no more direct description of our experience than that which uses these very words.[56]

ASPECT PERCEPTION AND INTERPRETATION

We have seen that the intrinsic nature of seeing something in accordance with an interpretation does not have an essence that is capable of being specified independently of the interpretation: the description using the terms of the interpretation is essential to the description of the intrinsic nature of the experience. But when we change from seeing something in accordance with one interpretation to seeing it in accordance with a different interpretation, do we really see differently or do we merely interpret what we see differently? This question is still undecided.

The principal consideration in favour of the view that what is seen is merely interpreted differently is the fact that in an important sense the 'optical picture', the 'visual picture' (das Gesichtsbild) remains the same.[57] What is the sense in which the

93

optical picture remains the same when an aspect is noticed? In the case of a two-dimensional arrangement of lines, a schematic representation of a cube, for example, the sense in which the optical picture does not alter when the lines are seen in accordance with one, and then another, interpretation is that the lines – their shapes, colours, size, and position – continue to be represented exactly as they were before the switch of aspect. Their appearance does not change in any way.[58] If we were asked to reproduce or indicate in some way the appearance of what we see, we would be right to draw or point to exactly the same arrangement of lines both times. Hence, there is a respect in which a change of aspect is not comparable to an apparent change in colour or shape. If the colour or shape of what we are looking at seems to change, we must indicate a differently coloured or shaped figure as reproducing the appearance of what we see on the two occasions.[59] In the case of a three-dimensional object, the sense in which the optical picture remains the same before and after an aspect is noticed is that the object continues to be represented in exactly the same way with respect to colour, three-dimensional shape, size, distance, and the relative distances of its parts from the perceiver – as when we see the likeness between one face and another (for example, our friend's old face in his new one).[60] This is just the three-dimensional analogue of the two-dimensional case. Again there is a lack of comparability of the aspect with any of the components of the representational content of the experience that are constant when an aspect of the three-dimensional object comes to be seen. In both cases it would seem that since the optical picture doesn't change, the change can only be one of interpretation.

Another important consideration in favour of the view that what is seen is merely interpreted differently when there is a switch in the interpretation in accordance with which it is seen is that seeing an aspect is subject to, or dependent on, the will:

> One wants to ask of seeing an aspect: 'Is it seeing? Is it thinking?' The aspect is subject to the will: this by itself relates it to thinking.[61]

In what sense is seeing an aspect subject to the will? Not in the sense that it is always responsive to our will.[62] For when we are seeing one aspect of an object and try to see another aspect we can fail; and when we try to hold an aspect constant it can change against our will. But although we can fail in our attempt to see, or hold constant, an aspect, the enterprise of trying to see a particular aspect of an object is always coherent and sometimes successful. Furthermore, in some cases we can change the aspect we see without being aware of any other act of volition that causes the change.[63] There is therefore a contrast between seeing an aspect of an object and seeing the object's colour or shape:

> It makes sense to say, 'See this circle as a hole, not as a disc', but it doesn't make sense to say 'See it as a rectangle', 'See it as being red'.[64]

An object is coloured and shaped in one particular way and when we see its colour or shape there is no question of our attempting to see it differently coloured or shaped. But an object can possess a number of aspects, and if we are seeing one of them we can try to see another.[65] Moreover, the fact that seeing an aspect is subject to the will[66] is an essential feature of seeing an aspect: it is essential to the concept of seeing an aspect that we can be asked to see a particular aspect, as we can be asked to form an image of something.[67] It is precisely because seeing an aspect, like forming an image,[68] is subject to the will that it does not 'teach us something about the external world'.[69] Seeing an object's colour or shape differs from seeing an aspect of the object in not being subject to the will, and, correspondingly, whereas the perception of colour or shape can instruct us about the external world, the perception of an aspect cannot provide comparable information.

It is this lack of comparability between noticing an aspect and seeing colour or shape that leads Wittgenstein to assert that what we perceive in the dawning of an aspect is not a *property* of the object. But if what we perceive is not a property (in Wittgenstein's sense), what is it? Wittgenstein's answer is that it is 'an internal relation between it and other objects'.[70] This is connected with his remark that 'if I am describing an aspect, the description the figure itself'.[71] A related point is that when we see the resemblance of one face to another, a human form in the lines of a puzzle-picture, a three-dimensional shape in a schematic drawing, and many other cases, we can be said to experience a *comparison*, since the immediate expression of the experience is the inclination to make a comparison between what we see and other objects.[72] Just as when we hear something as a variation on a particular theme[73] we must be inclined to compare the variation with the theme and can be said to hear a relation between the variation and the theme, so we must be prepared to relate a certain three-dimensional shape to a schematic drawing if we see that shape in the drawing. If we are not prepared to express our perception in terms of a particular interpretation, we cannot be said to perceive the aspect specified by the interpretation.

ASPECT PERCEPTION AND SEEING

What are the considerations that count against the idea that when we change from seeing something in accordance with one interpretation to seeing it in accordance with a different interpretation, we merely interpret what we see differently? These considerations will of course be those that are in favour of the view that we really *see* differently when a change of aspect occurs.

We have already seen that for Wittgenstein what is definitive of the notion of interpretation is that interpreting is an action or activity, and that it consists in making a conjecture or entertaining a hypothesis about what is seen – in the case of an illustration, a conjecture as to what it is intended to be. Both of these features of interpretation count against the idea that interpretation, and not seeing, constitutes the heart of a change of aspect. For, in the first place, any conjecture that we make may turn out to be false. Yet when we say that we see a figure as an F, or as the mirror-image of an F, there is no question of verification or falsification, any more than there is when we say that we see a bright red: 'I am seeing this figure as . . .' can be verified as little as (or only in the same sense as) 'I am seeing bright red'.[74] So there is a similarity in the use of the word 'see' when we talk of seeing an aspect and seeing a colour.[75] Secondly, whereas interpreting is an action, seeing is a state:

> The essential thing about seeing is that it is a *state*, and such a state can suddenly change into another one.[76]

And seeing an aspect is also a state[77] in this sense: like a visual impression, and unlike an interpretation or a thought, it has what Wittgenstein calls *genuine* duration: it can begin and it can end in a moment; how long it lasts can be determined by means of a stop-watch; whether it is still going on can be ascertained by spot-check.[78] So there is another significant similarity between the uses of the word 'see' in the two contexts: seeing an aspect resembles seeing a colour with respect to duration.

THE SOLUTION

We have now rehearsed the main considerations that count in favour, and also those that count against, the view that the intrinsic nature of our visual experience undergoes a change when we notice an aspect. But since there are considerations on both sides, how are we to resolve the issue whether a change in the interpretation in accordance with which we see something, or our beginning to see something in accordance with a certain interpretation, is really a matter of our seeing differently or our interpreting differently? The answer to the question should now be clear: the concept of seeing an aspect *lies between* the concept of seeing colour or shape and the concept of interpreting: it resembles both of these concepts, but in different respects.[79] In Wittgenstein's words:

It is seeing, *insofar as* . . .
It is seeing, only insofar *as* . . .
(That seems to me to be the solution.)[80]

There are ways in which the concept of seeing an aspect, seeing in accordance with an interpretation, seeing-as, resembles the concept of seeing a two- or three-dimensional coloured shape, but there are also ways in which the concepts differ.[81] If our conception of seeing is modelled upon the specific features of the perception of colour or shape, then seeing an aspect diverges from the model in this respect among others: when we 'see something different' – when there is an apparent change in colour or shape – the 'optical picture' changes, but when we experience a change of aspect the 'optical picture' does not need to undergo a comparable change. Seeing an aspect should not be forced into a mould that it conforms to only in some respects.

But the fact that it does not fit this particular mould does not imply that it is incorrect to think of us as *seeing* an aspect. For the correct use of the word 'see' is not restricted to the perception of coloured shapes, but covers seeing the resemblance of one face to another, seeing what is depicted in a picture, seeing the expression on a face as a smile or a posture as hesitant, seeing the look that one person casts at another, seeing a configuration of lines as a certain word, seeing one part of an illustration as figure and the other as ground, seeing two lines of a triangle as forming the apex and the third as base, and many other phenomena as well. The 'description of what is seen' covers a great variety of cases, and in particular it applies to visual aspects.[82]

On the other hand, the plain fact that it is perfectly in accordance with the normal use of the word 'see' to say that we see such varied phenomena carries no implication that the various concepts of seeing such different 'objects' of sight are uniform, and are of a piece with the concept of seeing a coloured shape. The claim that any description of what we see other than a description in terms of coloured shapes is an indirect description, replaceable in principle by a direct description in 'properly visual' terms – in terms of colour and shape – is certainly mistaken.[83] But it does not follow from the fact that there are numerous kinds of direct description of what we see, that the phenomena that answer to these descriptions are therefore as truly visual as colour and shape. Our normal way of expressing ourselves does not contain any *theory*, but only a *concept*, of seeing,[84] and the insistence that something that falls under one of the many descriptions of what is seen is really visual is empty in itself and misleading if it implies a comparison with the status of colour or shape. What is needed is an account of the resemblances and differences between the concept of seeing something that falls under one of these descriptions and other concepts of seeing – concepts of seeing something that falls under a different kind of description and especially a description solely in terms of colour or shape.[85] Wittgenstein emphasised the fact that there are 'hugely many interrelated phenomena and possible concepts'[86] within the field of perception, and that the smooth transition from one concept to another creates difficulties in philosophy because 'it is hard to understand and to represent conceptual slopes'.[87] The philosophical importance of the phenomenon of seeing an aspect derives from the fact that in the description of it the problems about the concept of seeing come to a head.[88] For its irreducibility either to a purely sensory or to a purely intellectual paradigm makes it especially suitable to promote recognition of the polymorphous character of the concept of seeing.

V

IMAGES, INTERNAL SPEECH, AND CALCULATION IN THE HEAD

TWO KINDS OF CONCEPT OF THE IMAGINATION

One group of concepts that it is difficult to obtain a reflective understanding of is a set of concepts concerned with activities of the imagination. These concepts have two essential features: they pertain to the imagination and they have an ostensible counterpart that involves either the exercise of one of the senses or the performance of a bodily action. On the one hand, there is the concept of visualising, or seeing in the mind's eye, and the allied concepts of imagining in perceptual modes other than sight (hearing in one's imagination, for example); on the other hand, there is the concept of internal speech, or speaking in one's imagination, the concept of calculation in the head and the allied concepts of performances in the imagination of activities that, when not performed in the imagination, involve external behaviour. The root of the problem raised by these concepts of the imagination is the nature of their relationships with their apparent counterparts. Each of these concepts seems to be the analogue in the realm of the imagination of a concept that runs parallel to it in the non-imaginative world. The problem is to elucidate the connection between the two concepts.

The difficulty assumes a somewhat different form in the two kinds of case I have distinguished. A concept of imagining in one of the perceptual modes is a concept of an experience, and the issue it raises concerns the relation between two concepts of experience: the concept of the imaginative experience and the concept of the kind of experience involved in the corresponding mode of perception. A concept of the performance in the imagination of an activity that can be performed outwardly raises the issue of the relation between the concepts of an outward and an inward performance of the same activity. In the first case, there are two kinds of experience and the question is how the one is related to the other. In the second case, there is a mental process and a form of behaviour and the question is how the 'inner' process is related to the outer process. Is the concept of the imagination in some way parasitic upon or derivative from its counterpart? If it is, can it be analysed in terms of it? If it is not, what degree of autonomy does it have? It is characteristic of Wittgenstein's treatment of psychological concepts that his investigation of these concepts of the imagination should go straight to the heart of the matter and concentrate upon the crucial issue of their relationship with concepts from which they appear to derive not just their life but their essential structure. He argues that the concepts of the imagination are dependent in a particular way upon the concepts of their counterparts, but that the experience of seeing in the mind's eye (for example) is intrinsically different from the experience of seeing, and the concept of internal speech should not be modelled on that of real speech. I begin with his account of the concept of imagining in a perceptual mode.

A SKETCH OF THE CONCEPT OF AN IMAGE

If we add to the outline of the concept of an image[1] in Wittgenstein's plan for the treatment of psychological concepts some points he makes elsewhere, we obtain the following sketch:

(i) Images are 'undergoings': they have duration and a course; they have intensity; they are not characters of thought.

(ii) Images are not distinguished from sensations by their 'vivacity'.

(iii) Whereas sensations teach us about the external world, images tell us nothing, either right or wrong, about the external world. (Images are not hallucinations, nor yet fancies.)

 (iv) Images are subject to the will.
  (v) It is just because forming images is a voluntary activity that it does not teach us about the external world.
 (vi) One cannot take an image for reality, nor things seen for things imaged.
(vii) While I am looking at an object I cannot imagine it. But when I am looking at an object, and seeing it clearly, I can visualise something else.
(viii) Difference between the language-games: 'Look at this figure!' and: 'Imagine this figure!'.
 (ix) Images are not pictures. I do not tell what object I am imagining by the resemblance between it and the image.
  (x) Asked 'What image have you?' one can answer with a picture.[2]

This miniature study of the concept is a paradigm of Wittgenstein's treatment of psychological concepts. What it tries to do is not to present an analysis, in the traditional sense, but to provide the basis for a perspicuous representation, which gives insight into the concept by making clear its essential connections with other concepts, and especially with the concept of seeing. Wittgenstein's guiding idea is that any philosophical puzzlement engendered by reflection on the concept can be dispelled by the elucidation of its relations with other concepts and the clarification of the criteria for the application of the concept, and it is to the achievement of this end that his picture of the concept is designed. What we need to examine is the accuracy of the picture, if it is elaborated in the manner Wittgenstein intended.

IMAGES, GENUINE DURATION, AND VIVACITY

Let us begin from the point that images and sensations (sense-impressions or sense-experiences) are united by their common possession of *genuine* duration. The significance of this feature in an account of the concept of perceptual imagery is that it enables the experience of images to be distinguished from capacities with which imaging is usually associated. If I can visualise somebody, then I will normally be able to describe the person's visual appearance (or perhaps to render it in some other way, by drawing, for example). Moreover, my capacity to describe the person in visual terms might begin at the moment at which I succeed in visualising him. This might suggest that the capacity to describe someone's visual appearance can be identified with the capacity to visualise him: each capacity is a manifestation of knowledge of what he looks like, and in each case there can be a sudden onset of the capacity. Wittgenstein invites us to imagine people who possess the capacity to represent in words or pictures the visual appearances of objects and who are familiar with the sudden onset of the capacity, but who never use such an expression as 'seeing in the mind's eye' and who deny the suggestion that they in some sense *see* the objects they can render in visual terms.[3] The question is whether these people would really be visualising objects, despite their reluctance to use the word 'see' in a linguistic expression that has a use comparable to 'see in the mind's eye'. Wittgenstein also raises the related question how I know that other people, who are happy to use such an expression as 'see in the mind's eye', really form visual images, and do not merely possess the ability to render the visual appearances of objects in words or pictures.[4] The answer in both cases turns on the concept of genuine duration: visualising possesses the feature of genuine duration, and it is the presence or absence of an inclination to speak in ways indicative of genuine duration that determines whether people can be said to be visualising objects.

Now if images and sensations are both 'undergoings', the only possible difference between them *as* undergoings would be a matter of degree – degree of intensity. It is something like this idea that is rejected by Wittgenstein when he denies that images are distinguished from sensations by their 'vivacity'. The thesis that images are distinguished from sensations by their vivacity claims that the essential difference between visualising a beech tree and the experience of seeing or hallucinating one, or between hearing the opening bars of Beethoven's fifth symphony in one's imagination and the experience of hearing them in the concert hall, is that the first experience is less vivid or lively than the second. But despite its distinguished ancestry, it is difficulty to give the thesis a sense that renders it plausible. It is true that images, like descriptions, can be indefinite, as when I visualise Jack without visualising him either as having blue eyes or as having non-blue eyes; and it is also true, as Wittgenstein indicates, that I can see one object and at the same time visualise another, so that my image does not obscure the object seen. But neither of these facts is sufficient to establish a credible sense for the thesis. And if we take the thesis at face value, understanding the vivacity of a visual experience as a function of the degree of apparent brightness, saturation of colour, definiteness of outline, clarity or sharpness of focus, and so on, it is open to a twofold objection: (i) To any experience of the one kind there corresponds a possible experience of the second kind that matches it with respect to vivacity in every respect, and (ii) The vivacity of what is seen can be *less* than that of what is visualised. For, in the first place, for any given specification of the vivacity of the visible properties of an array of material objects as observed from a particular point of view, it is possible both to see and to visualise such an array. And, secondly, I might on one occasion see a dimly lit object of uncertain shape and on another occasion visualise a brightly coloured object in good light. Hence the distinction between images and sensations cannot be explained in terms of vivacity.

THE SUBJECTION OF IMAGES TO THE WILL: NEGATIVE CONSIDERATIONS

We have already seen that in his sketch of the concept of an image Wittgenstein proposes to distinguish images from sensations by reference to whether they teach us about the external world: a logical criterion[5] for an experience to be included in the class of sense-experiences is that it should provide information, right or wrong, about the external world, whereas an image tells us nothing about the external world. This criterion is explained in terms of the notion of voluntariness or 'subjection to the will': images are subject to the will or voluntary (in a certain way), sensations are not,[6] and it is just because images are subject to the will that they do not instruct us about the external world. It is crucial that this notion of subjection to the will should be understood in the sense Wittgenstein intended if his proposal is to be assessed properly.

When Wittgenstein characterised images, the imagination,

imaging, as voluntary or subject to the will he did not mean that images are always produced by and responsive to the will. On the contrary, he recognised that images can occur against our will and be resistant to it, remaining with us when we would rather be without them.[7] So the doctrine that images are voluntary should not be interpreted to mean that each instance of visualising (for example) occurs voluntarily in the sense that the existence and continuation of our image is determined by our will. Wittgenstein was aware that his characterisation of imaging as subject to the will might encourage a particular form of this misinterpretation, which construes the connection with the will to refer merely to the machinery that produces or changes what is imaged:

> To say that imaging is subject to the will can be misleading, for
> it makes it seem as if the will were a kind of motor and the
> images were connected with it, so that it could evoke them, put
> them into motion, and shut them off.[8]

But if the voluntariness of imaging does not consist in its agreement with our will, what is to be understood by it? One suggestion is that Wittgenstein's view amounts to nothing more than the claim that imagining can be done intentionally, and that consequently it is open to the objection that it is unenlightening:

> *any* type whose canonical description does not imply that it is
> not intentional is something whose instances *can* in some
> conceivable circumstances be intentional: we learn little about
> something by being told that it can be done intentionally.[9]

But this objection is misplaced, for the claim that imagining can be done intentionally does not capture the content of Wittgenstein's characterisation of imaging as subject to the will. The assertion that visualising, for example, can be done intentionally amounts to no more than the proposition that some possible instances of visualising are intentional. I will argue, however, that Wittgenstein understands subjection to the will as being an *intrinsic* property of the state of visualising. Hence, 'subjection to the will' does not refer either to (i) an extrinsic feature of each experience of visualising (the way in which it has been brought about, is maintained, altered and brought to an end), or to (ii) a feature of only some possible instances of visualising.

Wittgenstein's main target in his examination of the concept of visualising is in fact the view that the essential difference between visual images and impressions is not based on any difference in the intrinsic properties of the states of visualising and seeing. He opposes the idea that seeing and visualising involve the same state of consciousness, an instance of this state counting as a visual impression when not directly under the subject's control (in virtue of having been brought about and caused to continue by the action of the external world), but an image when under his direct control: impressions differ from images only in their resistance to regulation by the subject's will. Wittgenstein concedes that there is a sense in which the 'experiential content' of seeing and visualising can be said to be essentially the same.[10] For a painted picture can represent equally what one sees and what one visualises; and descriptions of what is seen and what is visualised are of the same kind, a description fitting the one just as much as the other. So if I form an image of a face exactly as it looks and then see it later, my impression and my image have the same experiential content in the sense that the representation of the one – whether in words or pictures – is also the representation of the other. But it does not follow from this that the difference between visualising and seeing is that visualising involves the voluntary creation and continuation of the same kind of state that is experienced involuntarily in seeing. It is because the thesis that an impression and an image have the same experiential content might be thought to carry the implication that there is no intrinsic difference between the states of seeing and visualising that Wittgenstein suggests it might be better to avoid speaking of the states as having the same experiential content.

One line of attack Wittgenstein pursues against the idea that impressions differ from images only in not being under the subject's immediate control takes the form of questioning whether it is conceivable that we should be able to banish visual impressions and summon them before our minds, as we can images.[11] His initial point is that if this really made sense, it would follow that impressions could not inform us about the external world: objects would not have colours if we could see them coloured as we wished. But this immediately leads to the conclusion that in the imagined situation there would not be any

106

impressions, only images. Wittgenstein's more fundamental point is that the supposition of a state of affairs in which there would only be images and no impressions is senseless. This is certainly true, but it does not follow from the absurdity of this hypothesis that it is mistaken to think of there being an element common to seeing and visualising, such that (i) instances of it can be voluntary and instances can be involuntary, and (ii) an instance constitutes visualising when and only when it is voluntary (where an instance is voluntary if it is created, and has its course determined, by the will). The senselessness of the hypothesis implies only that it is not possible that all or most instances of the supposed common state should be voluntary. Hence this line of attack against the claim that there is a common element of the states of seeing and visualising, which is involuntary in seeing but voluntary in visualising, fails.

Now if this view were true, an experience of visualising and an experience of seeing might be intrinsically indistinguishable, and the essential difference between the two states could only be (it would seem) a matter of the machinery at work.[12] We have seen that Wittgenstein held that the distinction between images and impressions cannot be drawn in terms of vivacity. If the distinction between visualising and seeing is due to an intrinsic difference between the two kinds of state, Wittgenstein must identify an intrinsic property that one of the states possesses and the other lacks. Subjection to the will is intended to be the distinguishing mark.

THE SUBJECTION OF IMAGES TO THE WILL: THE POSITIVE ACCOUNT

There are three related ways in which Wittgenstein explains the idea that images are voluntary or subject to the will. The first is that imagining is something one can be told to do:

> If I say that imaging is subject to the will that does not mean that it is, as it were, a voluntary movement, as opposed to an involuntary one. For the same movement of the arm which is now voluntary might also be involuntary. – I mean: it makes

sense to order someone to 'Imagine that', or again: 'Don't imagine that'.[13]

The second way of explaining the idea is that the concept of imaging is akin to the concept of an action:

> I believe that if you do compare imaging with a bodily movement like breathing, which sometimes happens voluntarily, sometimes involuntarily, then you mustn't compare a sense impression with a movement *at all*. The difference is not that the one takes place whether we will it or not, whereas we control the other. Rather, one concept resembles that of an action, the other doesn't. The difference is more like that between seeing my hand move – and knowing (without seeing it) that I am moving it.[14]

> Forming an image of something is comparable to an activity. (Swimming.)[15]

> The concept of imaging is rather like one of doing than of receiving. Imagining might be called a creative act. (And is of course so called.)[16]

The connection between the first and second ways, and the provisional nature of the joint explanation, is signalled by this remark:

> Granted, there is a certain relationship between imaging and an action which is expressed in the possibility of ordering someone to perform either; but the *degree* of this relationship has yet to be investigated.[17]

The third way of explaining the idea that images are subject to the will invokes the attitude of observation:

> A principal mark that distinguishes image from sense-impression and from hallucination is that the one who has the image does not behave as an observer in relation to the image, and so that the image is voluntary.[18]

> When we form an image of something we are not observing. The coming and going of the pictures is not something that *happens* to us. We are not surprised by these pictures, saying 'Look!' (Contrast with e.g. after-images).[19]

If one says 'Imagination has to do with the will' then the same connection is meant as with the sentence 'Imaging has nothing to do with observation'.[20]

Wittgenstein's basic thought about the concept of imaging seems to be that imaging is something that someone does (an action), rather than something that merely happens to him (a passion), whereas the concept of seeing, unlike that of looking (an action), is the concept of something that happens (a passion), so that the attitude of the person who is imagining is not that of an observer, waiting attentively for changes to be brought about in him by the external world;[21] and the index of the fact that imaging falls on the active side of the active-passive divide is that it makes sense to try to form or banish an image and to order someone to imagine or not to imagine something, so that the verb 'imagine' can be used in the imperative mood. This idea, whatever its merits, is not vulnerable to the objection that I can visualise against my will. For although it is true that images can beset me against my will and remain, refusing to be banished, it does not follow that in such a case I am not active (in Wittgenstein's sense) and something is merely happening to me. The fact that I cannot prevent myself from doing something does not imply that what I do must be assimilated to an event in which I play an entirely passive role. Consider an analogous situation that requires an active-passive distinction: on one occasion I cannot get to sleep because, against my will, I cannot stop thinking about an important matter, on another occasion because of a severe pain in my knee. My thinking about the matter, unlike my experience of pain, is something I do, even though I do not want to be doing it. Or suppose I cannot tear my eyes away from a horrifying scene: my looking does not thereby become an event of the same order as my seeing. It is, however, notoriously difficult to capture the distinction between mental activity and passivity, and it is a question for further investigation whether Wittgenstein's account of the distinction will achieve what he intends.

THE DISTINCTION BETWEEN VISUALISING
AND SEEING

If this interpretation of Wittgenstein's investigation of the concept of visualising is correct, his opposition to the view that the experiences of visualising and seeing have a common element, which is voluntary (controlled by the will) in visualising, but not voluntary in seeing, becomes clear. For his claim is that it is definitive of the experience of visualising that our attitude when we visualise is not one of observation (unlike the experience of seeing). Hence it is wrong to think of visualising as a matter of the direct evocation of an experience of the kind we have when we are seeing. For this overlooks the fact that the two experiences are of incompatible kinds. It is not possible that our experience should be both one in which we adopt an attitude of observation and one in which we do not – which is what it would need to be, according to Wittgenstein's account, if it were to be at once an experience of visualising and an experience of the same kind as the one we have when we see.

The result is the same if we substitute the idea that visualising is an action for the idea that one who visualises does not behave as an observer in relation to his image. For there is a contrast between visualising and seeing in the crucial respect: visualising is an action, but seeing is a passion.[22] Now I cannot be both active and passive with respect to the same element of my consciousness at the same time. Hence the distinction between visualising and seeing is not that visualising involves the voluntary creation and continuation of the same kind of state that is experienced involuntarily in seeing.

We can also use Wittgenstein's account of the distinction between the experiences of seeing and visualising to explain what might appear to be a curious feature of his sketch of the concept of an image. For it might seem problematic that when I am looking at an object, and seeing it clearly, I can visualise something else, but I cannot imagine the object where I see it. But the reason I cannot imagine an object while I am seeing it is that this would require my attitude to the experiential content of my experience both to be and not to be one of observation, or the appearance of the object in my experience to be both an action and a passion.

CONFOUNDING IMAGE AND REALITY

A main aim of Wittgenstein's investigation of the concept of visualising is to elicit the distinctive logical criteria of visual images and visual impressions. One of the issues that naturally arises in this investigation is whether it is conceivable that an image might be mistaken for an impression or an impression for an image. A number of related themes concerned with the resemblance between image and impression runs through Wittgenstein's discussion:

  (i) whether a visual image is *like* a visual impression,
 (ii) whether a visual image and a visual impression *look alike* (but behave differently),
(iii) whether the 'experiential content' of an image is essentially *the same* as that of an impression,
 (iv) whether visual images and visual impressions are *inner pictures*, which resemble one another.[23]

The reason for this is clear: if image and impression are intrinsically similar, it might be possible to mistake the one for the other; but if they are dissimilar, this might be a satisfactory explanation of the fact that one cannot be mistaken for the other. Wittgenstein maintains that the concept of visualising does not admit the possibility that someone might mistakenly believe he is seeing (or hallucinating) something when he is in fact visualising it or that he might mistakenly believe he is visualising something when he is seeing it.[24] But since there is a sense in which the 'experiential content' of an image and a corresponding impression is the same, he rejects the suggested explanation in terms of dissimilarity:

> The dagger that Macbeth sees before him is not an imagined dagger. One can't take an image for reality nor things seen for things imaged. But this is not because they are so dissimilar.[25]

Now Wittgenstein tests the idea that an image and an impression

111

differ only in the control we can exercise over them – and also the thesis that an impression could not be taken for an image – by imagining a situation in which it seems to someone that what he is in fact seeing is obeying his will. But he rejects as absurd the idea that the person might be deluded and believe that his visual impressions are images.[26] If Wittgenstein is right, there must be something intrinsic to the state of seeing, which is present even when what someone sees appears to obey his will, and which necessarily is missing when one visualises. It seems clear that for Wittgenstein this intrinsic feature is the attitude of observation, or the passivity, that is definitive of seeing (as contrasted with visualising), and which is present in the imagined situation even though what the person sees behaves just as he wants it to and so appears to be responsive to his will. Now if someone knows that every feature of his visual experience is a result of his seeing something, then the fact that what he sees appears to him to obey his will is not going to incline him to misinterpret his experience as visualising, not seeing. But there is a different possibility, which is demonstrated in a well-known experiment on imagery.[27] In this experiment a subject sits facing a smoked-glass screen on the wall and he is asked to imagine a certain kind of coloured object. A picture of the kind of object the subject is asked to imagine is projected from a hidden source behind the screen on to the screen. The edges of the picture are fuzzy and it makes small random movements. The result of the experiment is that the subject reports seeing a mental image of the required object when and only when the brightness of the picture projected on to the screen is above the threshold of vision, so that the subject sees the picture. He therefore mistakes the picture he sees for an image he has conjured up. The relevant dissimilarity between the subject of the experiment and the person in Wittgenstein's imagined situation is that the subject of the experiment is trying to visualise, whereas Wittgenstein's imagined person is not, and he knows that he is seeing. What the experiment shows is that a person is not an incorrigible authority on the successfulness of his attempt to visualise.

It is not clear that Wittgenstein would have rejected this conclusion. For he qualifies his assertion that it is senseless to suppose that someone might mistake an image for an impression or an impression for an image by distinguishing between two forms of visualising, one of which rules out the possibility of mistake, the other allowing for it:

> But must one not distinguish here: (a) forming the image of a human face, for example, but not in the space that surrounds me – (b) forming an image of a picture on that wall over there? At the request 'Imagine a round spot over there' one might fancy that one really was seeing one there.[28]

This is the converse mistake of the one made in the experiment: the subject of the experiment takes what he sees for an image, whereas here one takes an image for reality. It is difficulty to think of a good reason for believing that the concept of visualising allows the one kind of mistake, but not the other.

IMAGES AND INFORMATION ABOUT THE EXTERNAL WORLD

Now that we have examined Wittgenstein's idea that images are voluntary or subject to the will, we can return to his proposal that images should be distinguished from sensations by reference to whether they teach us about the external world: a sensation provides information, right or wrong, about the external world, but an image tells us nothing about the external world – just because it is subject to the will. We have seen that the force of Wittgenstein's conception of images as being subject to the will is that it is definitive of the attitude of someone who is imaging that he is not behaving in the manner of an observer, who follows what happens with attention in order to find out what *does* happen. It would be wrong to understand his proposal as ruling out the possibility that we should obtain information about the external world through visualising: it would even be possible, with foreknowledge of what someone will visualise, to arrange a situation in which what he visualises provides him with accurate information about events as they happen. Wittgenstein's position is that when we visualise we are aware that our attitude is not one of observation, in which we look *at* something, so that we cannot be under the illusion that we are seeing or hallucinating: we know that we are not exercising our recognitional abilities, rightly or wrongly, to find out what is happening in the world about us, and that rather than receiving information about the world, we are engaging in a creative act that does not have a product whose existence is independent of our awareness.

IMAGES AND PICTURES

There is one last aspect of Wittgenstein's sketch of the concept of visualising that is worth attention. It concerns his rejection of the idea that images are pictures.[29] Now the assimilation of images to pictures could be more or less complete. The strongest claim would be that the concept of an image is the concept of a picture – an internal picture. But it is hard to take this claim seriously, for it is just a metaphor to speak of images as pictures in our minds and the distinguishing marks of images and pictures are both many and obvious. In so far as there is any temptation to think that an image is a picture, perhaps it arises from the invalid inference that since we are not seeing what we are visualising, we must be seeing something else, which stands for or is a representative of what we are visualising. It is easy to see how the view that images are pictures (or any other kind of inwardly visible object) is incompatible with Wittgenstein's condition that images are subject to the will. For if images were pictures, our awareness of them would come about by our *looking* at them, and this infringes the requirement that someone who visualises does not behave as an observer in relation to his image.

A weaker claim would be that the concept of visualising is more closely connected with the concept of seeing what is depicted in a picture than it is with the concept of seeing face to face, so that in one way images are more like pictures than other kinds of visible object. It is true that there is a respect in which the concepts of visualising and seeing what is depicted are alike and which is not possessed by the concept of seeing face to face. For when I visualise a man I might be visualising a particular man (Jack, say) or no man in particular; when I see a picture of a man it might be Jack whom I see depicted or no man in particular; but when I see a man I cannot be seeing no particular man. But this does not render the experience of visualising more akin to the experience of pictorial perception than to the experience of seeing (face to face). For when I hallucinate a man, I might not hallucinate any particular man (Jack say). Since the experience of seeing occurs not only when we see something as it is, or when we see something but see it wrongly (a fancy, in Wittgenstein's language), but also when we see nothing but undergo the experience as of seeing something (an hallucination), the experience of seeing what is depicted is no better model for the experience of visualising than the experience of seeing face to face.

Now Wittgenstein appears to give a bad reason for saying that images are not pictures. He asserts that I do not tell what object I am imagining by the resemblance between it and the image.[30] But neither do I tell what object is depicted in a picture by the resemblance between it and the picture. Since Wittgenstein was fully aware of this fact about pictures, it is puzzling that he should seem here not to do justice to it. We do not need, however, to solve this problem of interpretation in order to understand Wittgenstein's account of the sense in which Jack, say, is the person I am imaging. If I visualise Jack, I have formed an image *of Jack*, not because Jack resembles my image, or resembles it better than anyone else does, but because Jack is the person I understand myself to be imagining. In this way, Wittgenstein remarks, the concept of visualising is like the concept of depicting: my picture is a picture of the person I intend it to depict.[31] Now it would certainly be necessary to qualify this criterion in a full treatment of the subject to take account of possible radical mistakes in my conception of a person's appearance; and just as there is more than one sense in which a picture that I paint can be said to be a picture of Jack, there is more than one sense in which an image that I form can be said to be an image of Jack. But Wittgenstein's account undoubtedly identifies the central sense in which a particular person or thing can be said to be the object I am visualising.

CALCULATION AND SPEECH:
INNER AND OUTER PROCESSES

I now want to turn to the other kind of concept of the imagination that I distinguished at the beginning of the chapter. This kind of concept is a concept of the performance in the imagination of an activity that, when it is not performed in the imagination, involves external behaviour. The two concepts I shall concentrate on are those of calculation in the head and inner speech. The philosophical problem about these concepts arises in the following way. The concept of calculation out loud or on paper (say) is such that someone calculates out loud or on paper only if he utters certain sounds or inscribes certain marks. These sounds or marks are signs that the person understands as signs for the numbers and arithmetical operations that are involved in the calculation as he performs it. Let us call these sounds and marks the vehicle of the calculation. The concept of speech is similar: someone speaks only if he makes noises that form words in a language – a language he is speaking. In both cases, the concept requires the subject to make happen something that falls under two kinds of description: (i) a description in physical terms of a perceptible process, and (ii) a description that interprets the stages of the process in terms of the calculation performed or the language spoken. For example, if I am to perform a complex calculation out loud it must be true *both* that I utter certain sounds *and* that I first perform this stage of the calculation, then another, until I reach the conclusion. Calculation out loud or on paper requires a vehicle: the concept demands that the calculation is embodied in a process that begins when the subject begins to calculate and that terminates when he reaches the conclusion. There is therefore a process that a calculation out loud or on paper *consists in*, in the sense that there is a process with a nature of its own that also satisfies the description in terms of the nature of the calculation performed. Similarly, when anyone speaks a process must occur which constitutes the speaking, in the sense that it has an independently specifiable nature but also satisfies the description in terms of what is said.

Now there are obvious connections between, on the one hand, the concepts of speech and calculation out loud or on paper and, on the other hand, their counterparts in the realm of the imagination – the concepts of calculation in the head and silent speech 'within'.[32] Perhaps the most notable similarity is that just as the concept of outward calculation or speech is the concept of an articulated event, so is the concept of calculation in the head or inner speech.[33] In each case, the concept is of something that

116

occurs within a stretch of time and that can be said to consist of stages or steps. If I am asked what happened when I spoke in my imagination, I will give the answer that I said such-and-such words (in that order). If I am asked what happened when I performed a certain complex calculation in my head, the answer I will give will be a recitation of the steps I took: 'First I multiplied seven by eight, then I added thirteen, and finally I divided by twenty three'. Furthermore, there is a moment at which I begin to calculate in my head or speak in my imagination, a moment at which I end, and a moment at which each step of the calculation or speech is completed; and these moments can be correlated one-to-one with the times at which the parts of an 'outer' event take place. The internal calculation or speech can therefore *accompany* an external event: my performing a calculation in my head, or my saying a sentence in the imagination, might be synchronised with your performing the same calculation out loud or on paper, or your speaking the same sentence.[34]

This encourages the idea that the two kinds of concept are on all fours, except that in the case of the concepts of the imagination the role of the vehicle of the calculation or speech is played by an *inner* process rather than an outward process.[35] Accordingly, there will be two kinds of description true of what happens when we speak or calculate in the imagination, one of which specifies the nature of the process that the inner speech or calculation consists in. Has this not already been conceded by the characterisation of calculation in the head and silent speech as articulated events? It is important to realise that this is not so.

In the first place, we should remind ourselves of a significant dissimilarity between the two kinds of concept. In the case of speech and calculation out loud or on paper, although it is unlikely that I will be mistaken about what is happening, there is room for mistake. For example, I can say something aloud without realising that I am doing so, and I can think I am speaking when, although I am intending to, I am not: the required vehicle of speech is not something about which I have infallible knowledge: its occurrence is logically independent of my impression that it is or is not taking place. But there is no room for error or ignorance about my inner speech: when I speak in my imagination, there is no possibility that I should say one thing but be under the impression that I am saying something else, or nothing at all; and I cannot be saying nothing in my imagination but be under the impression that I am speaking inwardly.

Hence the following picture of inner speech and calculation in the head will be forced upon us, if we attempt to construe them as much as possible on the model of their outward counterparts. When I calculate in my head or say something silently:

(i) something happens in me,
(ii) which I bring about,
(iii) which is the internal analogue of what happens and is brought about by me when I speak or calculate overtly,
(iv) which I have direct and infallible concurrent awareness of.

But there are many reasons why we should not be seduced by this picture. I shall mention four considerations that undermine its plausibility.

Firstly, let us consider silent speech. What is supposed to be the internal analogue of the sounds that constitute the vehicle of speech? It is certainly unnecessary that I should somehow produce sounds in my head that only I hear. Moreover, even if such sounds should occur when I speak in my imagination, they could not assume the role of the inner process, for I might misperceive them or be unaware of their occurrence. So the postulation of 'internal' sounds would not help us to answer the question. Furthermore, whatever else might be suggested as a surrogate sound and that might take place in my body will be in no better position than an actual sound to constitute the required inner process.

The second reason for believing that the picture of the inner process misrepresents the concept of inner speech or calculation in the head is that I am quite unable to say what the alleged inner process is, even though I am supposed to have an immediate and infallible awareness of it when it takes place in me. It is true that when I calculate in my head or engage in inner speech I will sometimes be able to give a non-trivial answer to the question, 'What happened in you when you performed the calculation, spoke the sentence silently?'. For I might be aware of some process in my body (subvocal movements of the larynx, for example) that took place when I exercised my imagination, or I might be aware that I performed the calculation in my head by

118

visualising a written calculation or by speaking inwardly. But when I speak in my imagination or calculate in my head I am not usually aware of any bodily occurrence that is simultaneous with my inner speech or mental calculation, and, more importantly, no such awareness is demanded by the concept of calculation in the head or inner speech. Moreover, if I am aware that I performed a calculation in my head by means of inner speech (to take the more interesting of the two possibilities), this will enable me to say what happened in me on that occasion only if I am able to say what happened in me when I said the words of the calculation in my imagination. Hence, if the question 'What happened in you?' is seeking for a different answer from the one that simply announces the steps of the calculation or the sequence of words, I am at a loss to know what to say. As Wittgenstein pointed out, the fact that I cannot give a satisfactory answer to the question might mislead me into thinking that the inner process is a specific indefinable experience.[36]

This last point is connected with the third consideration that counts against the accuracy of the picture of the inner process. For if the concept of calculation in the head or silent speech is the concept of a certain kind of inner process, the meaning of 'to say something in one's imagination' or 'to calculate in one's head' must be taught indirectly.[37] Since what happens in one person's imagination is not open to another's observation, the best that can be done in the way of teaching the words is that one person should guess when the right kind of process is going on in another, and by directing the subject's attention to this occurrence hope that he will give himself the correct private ostensive definition. But we have seen that nothing can be based on the idea of private ostensive definition.[38] Hence, the scepticism that is bound to be induced if we try to construe the concept of silent speech or calculation in the head on the model of the inner process, finishes by swallowing up not only our knowledge of what (if anything) another person does when by his own lights he speaks in his imagination or calculates in his head, but also our own understanding of the concept.

A final reason for distrusting the seductive appearance of the picture of the inner process emerges if we consider the fact that there are very few activities we speak of performing in the head or inwardly. I can calculate in my head or engage in inner speech, but I cannot sharpen a pencil, ride a bicycle, climb a mountain or turn a somersault in my head. In the case of these latter activities, the only sense in which I can perform them internally is that I can imagine myself performing them. Now an imagined somersault is not a kind of somersault, and an imagined conquest of a mountain requires no inward analogue of the climbing I would need to do if I were really to stand at the top of a mountain. The suspicion naturally arises that inner speech or calculation in the head does not consist in an inner process, analogous to the perceptible process that is the vehicle of speech or outward calculation. If this is right, the source of the temptation presented by the picture of the inner process is clear:

> When words in our ordinary language have prima facie
> analogous grammars we are inclined to try to interpret them
> analogously; i.e. we try to make the analogy hold
> throughout.[39]

The idea that silent speech is an inner process monitored by the infallible subject is an illusion generated by modelling the 'inner' concept on the 'outer'.

Wittgenstein tries to break the grip of the picture of the inner process as a correct representation of the grammar of 'to say something in one's imagination' and 'to calculate in one's head' in a number of ways. Two of these methods are highly characteristic of his approach to the philosophy of psychology. The first involves the construction of a concept that is designed to stand in an analogous relation to a familiar concept to that in which the concept of calculation in the head stands to the concept of external calculation, or the concept of inner speech to that of speech:

> Imagine *this* game – I call it 'tennis without a ball': The players
> move around on a tennis court just as in tennis, and they even
> have rackets, but no ball. Each one reacts to his partner's
> strokes as if, or more or less as if, a ball had caused his
> reaction. (Manoeuvres.) The umpire, who must have an 'eye'
> for the game, decides in questionable cases whether a ball has
> gone into the net, etc., etc. This game is obviously similar to
> tennis and yet, on the other hand, it is *fundamentally*
> different.[40]

Corresponding to the fact that the language-games concerning tennis and tennis without a ball are strikingly similar, although the games are fundamentally different, is the fact that 'in important ways, speaking in one's imagination cannot be compared to speaking, but our language-games with the two are similar'.[41] Tennis without a ball is described in terms of tennis with a ball and internal speech in terms of external speech; but just as it would be wrong to postulate an analogue of a ball in the game of tennis without a ball, so it is wrong to postulate an internal analogue of speech in the activity of speaking in one's imagination. It is unsurprising that Wittgenstein applies the illustration of the game of tennis without a ball not only to the concepts of inner speech and calculation in the head, but also to the concept of visualising,[42] for the inclination to postulate a faint internal copy of speech, for instance, is of the same kind as the inclination to construe images as inner pictures. The strategy is of course in no way probative. But it was not intended to be. Its purpose is merely to suggest the nature of the error that lies behind the temptation to think that I *read off* the description of my image from something I see, or the description of my inner speech from an inner process I monitor.

The second way in which Wittgenstein tries to loosen the hold of the picture of the inner process is by inviting us to imagine a particular natural history of the concept of calculation in the head, which involves a rather different manner of speaking than our own. So let us imagine a society that posses the concept only of 'external' calculation. One day a person is asked what the answer is to a certain arithmetical problem and he comes up with the answer after a short period of time during which he has remained still: he has not *calculated* the answer (according to their language). Suppose the person is asked how he knows the answer. If he were to say that he has calculated the result, the people in his society would rightly dismiss what he says as absurd, and he knows that it would be incorrect for him to say this. Instead, he utters a form of words that has no established use, something like 'I calculated it unreally', or 'I calculated it and didn't calculate it' (rather than 'I calculated it in my head'). Furthermore, corresponding to our own readiness to specify how far we have got in the calculation we are performing in our head, this person is inclined to say some such thing as 'I have just calculated unreally the sum of thirteen and fifty six'. We therefore have, on the one hand, his capacity to indicate steps of the calculation without doing any perceptible calculation, and, on the other hand, the utterance he is inclined to make ('I calculated it unreally', for example):

> The phenomena of the first kind *might* bring us to offer the graphic description: It's as if he calculated somehow and somewhere, and told us steps of this calculation.[43]

But his utterance (unlike our own 'I calculated in my head') is rather less likely to seduce us into taking this graphic description seriously and – for want of any better way of understanding his remark – to postulate an inner process as the counterpart to the perceptible process that is integral to the concept of calculation out loud or on paper. If we now imagine other members of the society coming to join this person in his novel use of words, we will have imagined a natural history of the concept of calculation in the head, in which members of the society are not taught to say that they have calculated in their heads, or even that they have without qualification calculated, and which discourages the assimilation of the concept of calculation in the head to the concept of calculation (in the primary sense).[44] The reason this imaginary natural history discourages the assimilation is that the introduction of the concept into the language is not based on the discovery or hypothesis that the original person has calculated somehow and somewhere; this is marked by the different form of his utterance; and so it is not necessary to 'look at calculating in the head under the aspect of *calculating*, although it has an essential tie-up with calculating'.[45] In this way, the idea that 'calculation in the head' designates an inner process akin to the outer process of calculation can be disposed of.[46]

Now Wittgenstein's setting his face against the picture of the 'inner process' is likely to provoke the accusation that he is denying the reality of anything other than *behaviour*. Wittgenstein took steps to forestall this misunderstanding:

> 'Are you not really a behaviourist in disguise? Aren't you at bottom really saying that everything except human behaviour is a fiction?' – If I do speak of a fiction, then it is of a *grammatical* fiction.[47]

But if now someone were to say: 'so after all, all that happens is that he *reacts*, behaves, in such-and-such a way,' – then here is a gross misunderstanding. For if someone gave the account: 'I in some sense *calculated* the result of the multiplication, without writing etc.' – was he talking *nonsense*, or did he make a false report? It is a different use of language from that of a description of behaviour.[48]

But if we dispose of the inner process in this way, – is the outer one now all that is left? – the language-game of description of the outer process is *not* all that is left: no, there is also the one whose starting point is the expression. Whatever way our expression may run; whatever the way, e.g., it relates to the 'outward' calculation.[49]

Wittgenstein's position is clear. The verbal expression, the 'utterance', of a calculation in the head, whatever form it takes – whether it is couched in the words 'I in some sense calculated', 'I calculated unreally', 'I did and did not calculate', or 'I calculated in my head' – is not read off an inner process. But it does not follow that it is used as a description of the subject's behaviour. And the grammatical fiction Wittgenstein speaks of is the idea that the expressions 'calculate in the head', 'silent speech', 'to remember', and 'sudden understanding',[50] for example, stand for inner processes, so that the way to explain their meanings is to point out or describe the nature of the occurrences they name.

It is because he denies that the picture of the inner process is a correct representation of the grammar of psychological words, that Wittgenstein repeatedly rejects as the wrong question, '*What happens when* one imagines something, speaks inwardly, calculates in one's head, remembers, thinks, suddenly understands, intends or interprets a definition in a certain way, directs one's attention to something . . . ?'.[51] If we are asked what happens, either we mention something that is not constitutive of the mental state or process in question, or our inability to say what does constitute it encourages the idea that it is a specific inner process, indescribable in other terms.

Wittgenstein's denial that the picture of the inner process is a reliable guide to the ways in which psychological words are used is also the root of his diagnosis of philosophical puzzlement about the mind and the accusation of behaviourism he was aware his thought would attract:

> How does the philosophical problem about mental processes and states and about behaviourism arise? – The first step is the one that altogether escapes notice. We talk of processes and states and leave their nature undecided. Sometime perhaps we shall know more about them – we think. But that is just what commits us to a particular way of looking at the matter. For we have a definite concept of what it means to learn to know a process better. (The decisive movement in the conjuring trick has been made, and it was the very one that we thought quite innocent.) – And now the analogy which was to make us understand our thoughts falls to pieces. So we have to deny the yet uncomprehended process in the yet unexplored medium. And now it looks as if we had denied mental processes. And naturally we don't want to deny them.[52]

If 'There has just taken place in me the mental process of calculating in my head . . .' means nothing more than 'I have just calculated in my head . . .', then Wittgenstein would not wish to deny that there is such a mental process as calculating in the head. For to deny the mental process would be to deny that anyone ever calculates in the head.[53] And what holds for calculation in the head, holds also for silent speech and all other mental states and processes. But the recognition that psychological terms do not stand for 'outer' processes (forms of behaviour) might be followed immediately by the assumption that mental states and processes have an immaterial composition, accessible only from the individual subject's point of view, so that they are 'inner processes'. It is the denial of this assumption – the assumption made by anyone who takes the first step along the path Wittgenstein identifies as leading to philosophical puzzlement about the mind – that is misrepresented as the denial of such a mental process as calculating in the head. The impression that Wittgenstein wants to deny the mental process of calculating in the head and wants to insist that all that happens is that people behave in a certain way, arises from his settled opposition to the picture of the inner process as a true indication of the way in which the expression 'to calculate in the head' is used.[54]

VI

THOUGHT AND INTENTION

THE RAMIFICATIONS OF THOUGHT AND INTENTION

Two of the psychological concepts Wittgenstein identified as
being widely ramified are those of thought and intention.
Accordingly, different kinds of use of the words 'think' and
'intend' can be distinguished, and it would be possible to mark
these different kinds of use by the employment of different
words:

> Remember that our language might possess a variety of
> different words: one for 'thinking out loud'; one for thinking as
> one talks to oneself in the imagination; one for a pause during
> which something or other floats before the mind, after which,
> however, we are able to give a confident answer.
> One word for a thought expressed in a sentence; one for a
> lightning thought which I may later 'clothe in words'; one for
> wordless thinking as one works.[1]

> There might be a verb which meant: to formulate an intention
> in words or other signs, out loud or in one's thoughts. This
> word would not mean the same as our 'intend'.
> There might be a verb which meant: to act according to an
> intention; and neither would this word mean the same as our
> 'intend'.
> Yet another might mean: to brood over an intention; or to turn
> it over and over in one's head.[2]

125

Now Wittgenstein's investigation of these concepts is informed by his awareness of the ways in which they branch and it is correspondingly difficult to trace his path. But this task is made easier by two facts. The first is that Wittgenstein's examination of the concept of intention is severely limited in scope: it is centred on the idea of intention in the sense of what someone meant at a certain time, and it covers primarily what the person intended by something he did at that time and (a subsidiary theme) what he intended to do immediately. The second is that the two concepts are alike in a number of ways and are open to similar misunderstandings, so that Wittgenstein often moves freely from one to the other. However, there are also significant differences between the concepts and there is a particular misconception of the concept of intention that Wittgenstein was concerned to combat, one which construes intention on the model of a certain form of thought. Perhaps the easiest procedure is to begin with the concept of thought and modulate to the concept of intention. The natural place from which to start is Wittgenstein's early conception of thought, for his later understanding of the concept stands out most clearly when seen against the background of his former conception.

WITTGENSTEIN'S EARLY CONCEPTION OF THOUGHT

When Wittgenstein wrote *Tractatus Logico-Philosophicus* his view of the relationship between thoughts and propositional signs appears to have been something like the following.[3] The sign with which a thought is expressed is a propositional sign. For this sign to be understood as a proposition, its sense must be thought out. To think out the sense of a propositional sign is to have a thought that represents the sense. A thought consists of psychical constituents of some kind that have the same sort of relation to reality as words, so that these elements correspond to the words of a propositional sign with which the thought is expressed: the thought represents the sense in virtue of the correlation of its constituents with objects in reality and the way in which its constituents are related to one another. Hence a propositional sign and the thought expressed with this sense are representations of reality in the same sense, and a thought is true only if the

126

structure of its elements agrees with the structure in reality of the combination of objects correlated with these elements. This is what Wittgenstein had in mind in 1916 when he wrote:

> Now it is becoming clear why I thought that thinking and language were the same. For thinking is a kind of language. For a thought too is, of course, a logical picture of the proposition, and therefore it just is a kind of proposition.[4]

Much of his later philosophy is directed against this seductive picture of the relationship between thoughts, signs and reality, and his opposition to this picture is radical, as will soon become clear.

THE EXPRESSION OF THOUGHT IN WORDS

Wittgenstein's investigation of the concept of thought and its relations with the concept of the production and awareness of signs is a highly complex set of variations on a small number of themes, and whilst his main negative points are easy to formulate, his positive suggestions are not always lucid. Let us begin with the concept of 'thinking out loud': the concept of the expression of thought in words in the sense of the utterance or inscription of a sentence the speaker understands and which he intends in its normal sense. Since sentences can be spoken with or without understanding (as when I utter first an English and then a Chinese sentence), a sentence someone utters might or might not be the vehicle of a thought. The question is, 'When is the utterance of a sentence the expression of a thought?', or, 'What more needs to be true of someone who expresses a thought in words than that he utters the words?'. Wittgenstein's principal negative thesis is that no process needs to take place when someone expresses a thought in words other than the production of the words, and any additional process that might occur would be redundant. Hence the concept of the expression of thought in words is not the concept of a double process. The fundamental consideration in favour of Wittgenstein's thesis is that no additional process would be sufficient in itself to turn a case in which someone utters words he does not understand into a case in which he utters the words with understanding. For example, any additional process that consists of a series of mental elements correlated with the elements of the sentence would simply duplicate language with something else of the same kind (as in Wittgenstein's early philosophy).[5]

Now the problem raised by the concept of the expression of thought in words also arises for the concept of the imagined expression of thought in words, and Wittgenstein's thesis can be extended to cover the case of internal speech or any other form of internal production or awareness of signs. Just as I can utter a sentence with or without understanding, I can speak a sentence silently with or without understanding. The difference between my engaging in inner speech on one occasion with and on another occasion without understanding is not that a certain process occurs in my consciousness in the former but not the latter case. It is true that when I express a thought in words, my thought is what I mean by the words, not the words themselves; and when I speak silently, my thought is again what I mean by the words, not the words themselves. But the difference between (internal or external) speech with and without understanding does not consist in a further process that accompanies speech when and only when it is understood. In neither internal nor external speech that I understand does there need to be anything in my consciousness other than the words themselves:

> When I think in language, there aren't 'meanings' going
> through my mind in addition to the verbal expressions: the
> language is itself the vehicle of thought.[6]

A CONSCIOUS INNER VEHICLE OF THOUGHT

Now when I express a thought in words, something must happen, which is the vehicle of the thought; and if I am aware that I have expressed the thought, I must be aware of the vehicle. Is it true, however, that if I think but do not express that thought, there must be an *internal* vehicle of thought; and must I be aware of this inner vehicle of thought when I think a thought which is unexpressed at the time? We have already seen that an 'inner process' involving the consciousness of signs is not sufficient in itself for me to think a thought (as when I engage in inner speech of sentences I do not understand), but that what is required to make this the vehicle of a thought is not an extra process. The question now is whether an unexpressed thought demands an inner vehicle I am conscious of in thinking the thought.

Let us consider a case in which I suddenly think a thought without expressing it: the thought that Jill is coming tomorrow suddenly occurs to me or I suddenly wonder whether I posted the letter to Jack, for example. Now I will be aware of the nature of my thought in the sense that I will be aware of what it is that I have thought: if I wanted to, I could express the content of the thought in words. But how do I know what its content is?

This question will seem to be an appropriate one if we model my awareness of my own thoughts on my awareness of another's thoughts. For my awareness of the content of my thought will then be dependent upon my awareness of the nature of the occurrence that constitutes my thinking the thought: it will be necessary that my thinking the thought consists in something, that I am aware of what happens when I think it, and that it is in virtue of this awareness that I am aware of what it is I think. I am aware of the content of another's thought only via an awareness of something other than that content: I must perceive the verbal expression of his thought, say, and I must understand it correctly. How could it be otherwise in my own case? Without an awareness of what happens when I think the thought – the internal embodiment or representation of my thought – I must be as ignorant of what I think as I would be of what another thinks if I were to be unaware of any perceptible sign of his thought. At least, this is how the matter will appear if we construe self-awareness on the model of other-awareness.

But the assumption of a conscious internal vehicle of thought would not solve the problem which leads to its introduction. If I am supposed to be aware of what happens in my mind when I think an unexpressed thought, and this is supposed to reveal to me what I think, what is the relation between my awareness of the nature of whatever it is that happens on a certain occasion when I think a thought and my awareness of the content of the thought? How is the content of my thought derivable from the happening that constitutes the occurrence of the thought? Is it possible for me to be unaware of what happens when I think a thought and so be unaware of the thought, or to be aware of the nature of what happens but to be unaware of the content of the

129

thought or to derive a wrong content (as it is in the third-person case)? Without soundly based answers to these questions, the postulation of a conscious internal vehicle of thought achieves nothing.

We have in effect already seen that whatever happens in my consciousness when I think a thought places no constraints on the content of my thought: the intrinsic nature of any happening is compatible with the occurrence of any thought (a thought with any content). For no awareness of signs and no other state of or process in consciousness is sufficient in itself for me to think a thought with a certain content. Hence the requirement that *something* must happen in my consciousness when I suddenly think a thought, and that my awareness of what I think (or even that I have thought something) is founded in my awareness of this happening, loses its appeal: it appears compelling only when it seems sufficient to explain my awareness of what I think. Of course, it does not immediately follow from the fact that the intrinsic nature of anything that happens in my consciousness is compatible with the contemporaneous occurrence of a thought with any content that the occurrence of a thought does not require a change in my state of consciousness, any more than it follows from the fact that any movement of my body is compatible with my then making any assertion that it would be possible for me to make an assertion without moving my body in any way. But although the possibility that the occurrence of a thought requires a change in consciousness remains open, there is no reason to accept it: thought is not dependent upon a conscious vehicle in the way that assertion is dependent upon a bodily movement vehicle.

This can be illustrated by any state of consciousness. Just as I can be seeing anything or nothing when I think a certain thought, so no image (of a word, for example) is necessary for me to think the thought and no image precludes me from thinking the thought. Furthermore, the occurrence of the thought does not require that some image or other should be before my mind. Likewise, when I think a thought I do not need to engage in an act of silent speech in which I utter a sentence in my imagination. Hence it is not only possible for a thought with a particular content to be variously realised or manifested in my consciousness, but there does not need to be *any* visible sign of it in my consciousness at the time I think the thought: nothing needs to be before, or to run through, my consciousness when I think. And since my thought need not be detectible in any way in my consciousness, it is not necessary for me to read off my thought from anything that happens there. Self-awareness should therefore not be modelled on other-awareness: my awareness of what I think is not mediated by an awareness of something that happens in my consciousness, which I interpret, rightly or wrongly, as the thought that I need to buy a new pair of shoes, for example.

We can therefore add to the conclusion that language is itself the vehicle of thought when I think in language, the further conclusion that I can think without speaking either outwardly or inwardly and without being aware in any other way of linguistic or non-linguistic signs. Hence, if I think a certain thought but do not think it in language either by 'thinking out loud' or by talking in the imagination, there need be no description available to me of what I have done other than 'I thought that *p*', where '*p*' specifies the content of the thought.

THE HARMONY OF THOUGHT AND REALITY

Light is thrown from another direction on Wittgenstein's investigation of the concept of thought by a consideration of his account of the thought-content of psychological states, which receives its fullest and clearest expression in his treatment of the topic of the agreement or harmony of thought and reality.[7] His examination of the idea that there is a kind of agreement between thought and reality has two principal aspects. The first appears to be trivial when considered in isolation. My thought, intention, expectation, wish, hope or command has a content that may or may not agree with reality: a thought can be true or false, an intention carried out or not acted upon, an expectation or a hope fulfilled or unfulfilled, a wish satisfied or unsatisfied and a command obeyed or disregarded. What is the connection between my thought, intention, expectation, wish, hope or command when reality agrees with it? To take the case of expectation: if my expectation is described as the expectation that *p*, the state of affairs that fulfills this expectation is described as the state of affairs that *p*:

> It seems as if the expectation and the fact satisfying the expectation fitted together somehow. Now one would like to describe an expectation and a fact which fit together, so as to see what this agreement consists in. Here one thinks at once of the fitting of a solid into a corresponding hollow. But when one wants to describe these two one sees that, to the extent that they fit, a *single* description holds for both.[8]

This is the sense of Wittgenstein's remarks, 'It is in language that an expectation and its fulfillment make contact'[9] and 'It is in language that wish and fulfillment meet'[10], and, generalising, of his remark, 'Like everything metaphysical the harmony between thought and reality is to be found in the grammar of the language'.[11] In the case of each kind of mental item, the content of an item of that kind and the fulfillment, satisfaction (or whatever) of the item, are rendered into language in the same words.

Moreover, a description of an expectation in terms of what is expected is an *internal* description of it, as it would not be if it were like a description of a state of hunger in terms of what might possibly remove it.[12] If an expectation is described in terms of what is expected, this is not an expression of a causal hypothesis to the effect that the occurrence of the state of affairs expected will make the expectation disappear. Neither does it express the conjecture that the occurrence of the state of affairs said to be expected will, if the subject is aware of it, give him an experience of some kind:

> Fulfillment of expectation doesn't consist in this: a third thing happens which can be described otherwise than as 'the fulfillment of this expectation', i.e. as a feeling of satisfaction or joy or whatever it may be.[13]

Hence the content of an expectation is not determined by something that happens at a later date, but is intrinsic to it. Furthermore, it is essential that there should be an internal description of an expectation, or any other mental state that can agree with reality, which specifies the content of the item. For if there were no internal connection between thought and reality, there would be no sense to the idea of the content of a thought.

Now this first aspect of Wittgenstein's treatment of the idea that there is some kind of agreement between thought and reality derives its significance from the second. For – to continue with the case of expectation – although my expectation and what happens when it is fulfilled are described in the same terms, the agreement between them is not a consequence of the fact that what happens was present in my expectation. That would not be possible. But if the agreement consists in the fact that if my expectation has a certain content, it follows that its fulfillment is described by the words that specify that content, the question arises, 'In virtue of what is it true that my expectation does have that content?'. And a similar question can be raised about my thought, intention, wish, hope or command. The second aspect of Wittgenstein's consideration of the problem of the harmony between thought and reality concerns the relationship between what happens when I think a certain thought, form a certain expectation, or whatever, and my thinking a thought with that content or forming that expectation. Consider a situation in which I am expecting someone:

> what's it like for him to come? – The door opens, someone walks in, and so on. – What's it like for me to expect him to come? – I walk up and down the room, look at the clock now and then, and so on. But the one set of events has not the smallest similarity to the other! So how can one use the same words in describing them? What has become now of the hollow space and the corresponding solid?[14]

SIGN, SHADOW, AND REALITY

Wittgenstein's main preoccupation with the issue of the content of mental states concerns the idea that something other than and essentially different from a mere sign must be present to my mind when I think, expect, intend, wish, hope or command in order for the requisite internal relation between me and reality to obtain. This illusion is by now familiar. It is encouraged by the undeniable fact that whatever signs do go through my mind, I could understand them in different ways and I could mean nothing by them. The mistake is to conclude that I can be the subject of a state with a thought-content only if the *sense* of the signs is also present to or goes through my mind. But nothing else that went through my mind would establish an internal relation of the required kind between me and reality. Any supposed intermediary in my mind connecting the expression of my thought in signs with the reality with which my thought is concerned – a 'pure intermediary between the propositional signs and the facts'[15] – will stand in no closer relation with reality than the signs themselves: a 'method of projection' will always be needed to effect the transition from what is in the mind to the reality it represents. And this difficulty cannot be overcome by the *specification* of a method of projection; for the specification of a method of projection will just be another sign, about which the same problem arises.[16] Hence nothing is gained by the postulation of a third item, which intervenes between the expression of my thought in signs and the reality with which my thought is concerned.[17]

This is true no matter how like reality we imagine the intermediary to be: the problem is not removed by making the intermediary a 'shadow' or copy of the object of my thought.[18] Wittgenstein held that the idea of a shadow as a constituent of my thought amounts to the idea that my thought contains a *picture* of the object of my thought:

> The shadow, as we think of it, is some sort of a picture; in fact, something very much like an image which comes before our mind's eye; and this again is something not unlike a painted representation in the ordinary sense . . . But it is absolutely essential for the picture which we imagine the shadow to be that it is what I shall call a 'picture by similarity'. I don't mean by this that it is a picture similar to what it is intended to represent, but that it is a picture which is correct only when it is similar to what it represents. One might use for this kind of picture the word 'copy'.[19]

But even if we make the intermediary into a picture by similarity, we run up against two related facts: it is possible for any picture by similarity to be understood in some other fashion, and there are pictures that are not pictures by similarity. The specification that an item is a picture by similarity merely adds a sign to the picture and the content of the combination of the picture and the sign raises the same problem as the picture considered by itself. Moreover, since there are pictures that are not pictures by similarity (as in the case of a plane projection of one hemisphere of the Earth),[20] any picture is susceptible of interpretation as a picture *not* by similarity, so that what the picture represents cannot be read off the picture unless a particular rule of projection is assumed.[21] Hence the assumption of a shadow as a constituent of my thought does not endow it with a content it would otherwise lack:

> If we keep in mind the possibility of a picture which, though correct, has no similarity with its object, the interpolation of a shadow between the sentence and reality loses all point. For now the sentence itself can serve as such a shadow.[22]

The fact that correctness of representation is relative to method of projection undermines the idea that the content of thought must be ensured by some kind of simulacrum of the content being present as a constituent of the thought.[23]

Now the realisation that whatever signs I am aware of, they can be understood in different ways, and that the postulation of any accompaniment of or replacement for a sign does not solve the problem of interpretation, can make it appear that no matter what happens in my mind at a certain time, I cannot then be connected with reality in the way that is required if I am to be the subject of a psychological state which possesses a thought-content. But the truth is that there are facts about me other than facts about conscious occurrences in my mind, and these can make it correct to ascribe to me a psychological state with a certain thought-content, thereby making it possible for there to be the required harmony (or lack of harmony) with reality.

THE PROBLEM OF INTENTIONAL REPRESENTATION

Let us begin with a number of Wittgenstein's illustrations in which the thought-content is about a particular individual. When we are puzzled by the question, 'What makes my image an image of Jack?', we can suffer from the temptation to think that unless Jack is introjected into my image, or (as second-best) unless a surrogate, a shadow, of Jack is present in my mind, my image cannot be an image of Jack. But we have seen that this is an unnecessary shuffle. If I have an image in my mind, what makes it true that my image is an image of Jack is not the nature of the image as specified in spatial and coloured terms and the similarity of the image so specified to Jack, but instead the fact that Jack is the person I understand myself to be imagining.[24] Likewise, if what passes before my mind is a series of words, what makes it true that I have at this moment thought of Jack is not any intrinsic features of the signs that go through my mind when I think of him. What occurs in my mind is describable in the way it is – as an image, or the expression of a thought, of Jack – in virtue of facts other than the state of my consciousness, and, in particular, in virtue of my mastery of a language, my past and present situation, and what I would do.[25] The importance of these considerations is underlined by Wittgenstein in the following example:

> 'At that word we both thought of him'. Let us assume that each of us said the same words to himself – and how can it mean MORE than that? – But wouldn't even those words be only a *germ*? They must surely belong to a language and to a context, in order really to be the expression of the thought *of* that man. If God had looked into our minds he would not have been able to see there whom we were speaking of.[26]

Now in *Philosophical Grammar* Wittgenstein states that the whole problem of representation is contained in 'That's *him*' (this picture represents *him*), where the picture depicts him in the sense that he is the person it is *meant* to represent.[27] The problem is to explicate the notion of intentional representation. But in order to understand the grammar of 'intentional representation' it is necessary to ask, What counts as a criterion for someone's intending a picture to be a picture of N?[28] Wittgenstein's answer to this question is that perhaps the person says that it is a picture of N or writes N's name underneath the picture. And he maintains that when I form an image of N:

> The image of him is an unpainted portrait.
> In the case of the image too, I have to write his name under the picture to make it the image of him.[29]

He later explains that he does not mean that I must imagine both N and his name at the same time and he asserts that my understanding the image as N's is not something that happens when I imagine him. When I imagine N nothing needs to be *present* except my image: what *precedes* or *follows* the imagining may connect the image with N.[30] I understand the image as N's but my interpretation is not a contemporaneous occurrence:

> the interpretation isn't something that accompanies the image; what gives the image its interpretation is the *path* on which it lies.[31]

Wittgenstein's negative thesis that an interpretation does not determine meaning is one of the main topics of Chapter II and it is unnecessary to elaborate upon it here. But his positive account of meaning and intention in intentional representation as it has been sketched above is far from clear and it might easily be misunderstood. There is a lack of clarity about the idea of the *path* on which an image is said to lie. And Wittgenstein's emphasis on the fact that my intention is not an experience, not an accompaniment of my image, not a process, and his insistence that the connection between my image and a particular person need not be present when I visualise but may be established by what happens before or after,[32] might encourage the idea that Wittgenstein is arguing that the connection with the person imagined does not exist, or at least need not exist, at the time in question. But this would be a misrepresentation of his position, as I shall now try to show.

INTENTIONAL REPRESENTATION: THE SOLUTION

Wittgenstein returned to the topic of intentional representation in imagery many times. *Last Writings on the Philosophy of Psychology* contains some of the clearest and most explicit formulations of his positive conception. Consider this passage:

> What makes my image of him into an image of *him*?
> When I say 'I'm imagining him now as he . . .', then nothing is being designated as his portrait.

But can't I discover that I pictured him quite wrongly? Isn't my question like *this*: 'What makes this sentence a sentence that has to do with *him*'?
'The fact that we were speaking about him.' – 'And what makes our conversation a conversation about *him*?' – Certain transitions we made or would make.[33]

Here Wittgenstein likens the question 'What makes my image of him into an image of *him*?' to the question 'What makes our conversation a conversation about *him*?', and he answers the second question by reference to the transitions we made or would make. In previous examples of similar kinds[34] he has referred to 'the chain of interpretations, of explanations' and the 'connections that one would or would not make', and what he has in mind is illustrated here:

'Who were you talking about?' – 'About N.' – 'About my friend N.' – 'About the person in this photograph.' – 'About the person who is just coming through the door.'[35]

The issue of intentional representation in imagery comes to a head in section 843:

Here, as in many related cases, there is something we might call a *germinal experience*: an image, a sensation, which *grows* little by little into a full-fledged explanation. And one feels inclined to say that it is a *logical* germ, something which had to develop the way it does out of *logical* necessity.
On a particular occasion I suddenly think of a certain person. How did it happen? – I saw a picture before me, maybe only grey hair – then I said, I see N before me (but it is still possible that many other people have that name). – But then I explain I meant *that* N. who . . ., etc. – Moreover, I didn't *read* the name *in* the mental image, and neither did I subsequently *interpret* it thus and so. For if I'm asked whether it was only later that I knew or decided to whom the grey hair and the name N. belonged, then I shall say no, that I knew it from the beginning. But knowing is not an experience. – 'I knew it from the beginning' really only means: I didn't read the name off the picture, for I didn't think 'Whose hair is this?' or 'Who looks like this?' – nor did I say to myself 'For now, let's let the name

'N' stand for *this* person'. It could be said that I became more and more explicit.
But then where does the idea of the logical germ come from? Which really means: Whence the idea that 'Everything was already there from the beginning and was contained in the initial experience'? Isn't the reason for this similar to James's claim that the thought is already complete when the sentence begins? This treats the intention like an experience.
I advance from explanation to explanation. But I only seem to say what was there from the beginning. Of course. For 'It hasn't been there from the beginning' would be wrong.
'The thought is *not* complete from the very beginning' means: I didn't find out or decide until later what I wanted to say. And *that* I do *not* want to say.

Wittgenstein believes that when I think of someone it will often, but not always,[36] be the case that I am aware of something happening in my consciousness: I might be aware of a word, an image, or various other things.[37] What I am aware of he refers to as a germ or seed.[38] The question at issue is the relation between the germ and my awareness of the content of my thought, which I may later express in words by means of a series of explanations. In the above passage Wittgenstein considers a case in which I am aware of an image when I think of someone and he makes a number of connected points about thought and intention that are not restricted to intentional representation in imagery. The first is that when I visualise someone and say that it is N whom I am visualising, I do not read off the person's name from my image. The second is that my awareness that I am visualising N is not a subsequent interpretation of the image, but existed all along. The third is that my awareness is revealed or expressed in the (sincere) answers I would give to questions about who it is that I have visualised. The fourth is that it does not logically follow from a description of the intrinsic nature of what happens in my consciousness (the germ) that these are the answers I *should* give to these questions. The final point is that my thought or intention – my thinking of N, my meaning N by my image – is not an experience, a happening in my consciousness.
These points are repeated in the related cases he considers: my intention to continue an interrupted sentence in a certain way,

my meaning one thing rather than another by what I say, my writing to or speaking of a certain person, and many others. Here is a clear example:

> He asks 'What did you mean when you said . . .?' I answer the question and then I add: 'If you had asked me before, I'd have answered the same; my answer was not an *interpretation* which had just occurred to me.' So had it occurred to me earlier? No. – And how was I able to say then: 'If you had asked me earlier, I'd have . . .'? What did I infer it from? From nothing at all. What do I tell him, when I utter the conditional? Something that may sometimes be of importance.
> He knows, for example, that I haven't changed my mind. It also makes a difference whether I reply that I was 'only saying these words to myself' without meaning anything by them; or, that I meant this or that by them.[39]

In *Philosophical Investigations* Wittgenstein considers a number of cases in which I mean something and then say what it is that I meant, and he raises the question whether my words report an existing connection with what I meant or establish a connection with it that did not exist before:

> What is there in favour of saying that my words describe an existing connexion? Well, they relate to various things which didn't simply make their appearance with the words. They say, for example, that I *should have* given a particular answer then, if I had been asked. And even if this is only conditional, still it does say something about the past.[40]

It is clear, I believe, that the second aspect of Wittgenstein's consideration of the harmony between thought and reality, which involves explaining the idea of the thought-content of psychological states, makes essential reference to the inclinations, dispositions, and capacities of the subject of a psychological state that possesses a thought-content, and so to what he *would* do, rather than to the state of his consciousness. A special significance is assigned to how someone would express his psychological state in words: a criterion for which person my picture, image, sentence, or thought is of, or for what I intended to say, or for what I meant by what I said, is the answer I would have given to a question about my meaning. Now Wittgenstein is always circumspect in the answers he gives to questions about the criteria for someone's being in a psychological state with a thought-content, for there is no single criterion and the criterion he wishes to stress – the subject's verbal expression of his state – needs to be formulated in conditional terms which involve an ineliminable reference to the state in question. Furthermore, the criterion of the subject's verbal expression of his state pre-supposes the psychological concepts that lie at the heart of Wittgenstein's investigation of language and thought, the con-cepts of meaning, intention, and thought-content. Consider a case in which I am interrupted in speaking and I later report how I was going to continue my sentence. My later report constitutes good evidence only if, firstly, I have not forgotten my intention and, secondly, the content of my report (what I mean by the words I utter) is that this was my intention; and if I remember accurately the way I intended to continue, I would have continued in this way only if nothing happened to prevent me from doing so and I did not abandon my intention.

Nevertheless, the fact that my verbal expression of a state of one of the kinds Wittgenstein focuses upon – intention, thought, image, expectation, hope and wish – is a criterion for the content of the state enables Wittgenstein to dissolve the problem of my knowledge of the content of my state:

> How do I know that this picture is my image of the *sun*? – I *call* it an image of the sun. I *use* it as a picture of the *sun*.[41]

> Where are we to find what makes the wish *this* wish, even though it's only a wish? Nowhere but in the expressed wish.[42]

> What it always comes to in the end is that without any further *meaning* he *calls* what happened the wish that that should happen.[43]

> By nature and by a particular training, a particular education, we are disposed to give spontaneous expression to wishes in certain circumstances. (A *wish* is, of course, not such a 'circumstance'.) In this game the question whether I know what I wish before my wish is fulfilled cannot arise at all. And the fact that some event stops my wishing does not mean that it fulfills it. Perhaps I should not have been satisfied if my wish had been satisfied . . . .

141

Suppose it were asked 'Do I know what I long for before I get it?'
If I have learned to talk, then I do know.[44]

The question whether and how I know what I expect, say, fails to
arise, for the sentences 'I don't know whether I'm expecting Jill
to come today or Jack to come in three days time' and 'He
believes he's expecting Jill to come today but in fact he's
expecting Jack to come in three days time' are senseless and the
content of my expectation is just what I take it to be (what my
verbal expression of it would represent it as).[45] Moreover, my
verbal expression is a criterion not only for the content of the
state, but also for the psychological category of the state: it would
be senseless for me to assert that I don't know whether I'm
expecting Jill to come, *wishing* that she had come, *hoping* that she
will come, *thinking* of the possibility of her coming, *recalling* the
last time she came . . . , and which of these conditions I am in is
the one I take myself to be in. Hence the problem of self-
awareness vanishes under this conception of my verbal expression
as a criterion for the nature of my psychological state.

Now it might be thought that Wittgenstein's emphasis on my
verbal expression as definitive of the nature and content of my
psychological state assigns an unwarranted primacy to the verbal
expression. But this would be to ignore the other side of
Wittgenstein's account. As in the case of sensation, so for
psychological states with a thought-content, Wittgenstein ties the
verbal expression of the state to the non-verbal behaviour-criteria
for the presence of the state:

> What is the natural expression of an intention? – Look at a cat
> when it stalks a bird; or a beast when it wants to escape.
> ((Connexion with propositions about sensations.))[46]

There are criteria for whether I understand the verbal expression
of intention or expectation, for example, and these criteria relate
to my behaviour and circumstances: my understanding of the
verbal expression is founded on a continuing correlation between
the way in which I would give verbal expression to my condition
and other ways, indicative of my intention or expectation, in
which I do or would behave. If we imagine this connection
broken, my utterance would no longer be a verbal expression of
intention or expectation and so would not count as a criterion for

my psychological state. The reason Wittgenstein does not attempt to list the other criteria for intention and expectation is that no such list could be drawn up: there are indefinitely many ways in which my expectation or intention might be manifested in my behaviour during the time my expectation or intention lasts, and indefinitely many ways in which I might react when my expectation is fulfilled or unrealised or my intention is forgotten, abandoned, or prevented from issuing in action. But the fact that there can be no such list fails to count against the manifestly correct idea that my understanding of the language of intention and expectation is rooted in a correspondence between the occasions on which I would be able to give sincere verbal expression to my intention or expectation and those when it would be true to attribute an intention or expectation with that content to me, as this could be revealed by my behaviour in innumerably many ways.

Wittgenstein's emphasis on the verbal expression of intention, expectation, wish, thought and hope, for example, is therefore fully compatible with the attribution of such states to creatures that lack a language. But the kinds of psychological state attributable to languageless creatures and the limits and specificity of the possible thought-contents of states of a languageless creature or someone who possesses only a primitive language is a matter for further investigation – an investigation Wittgenstein did not pursue in any detail.[47]

THOUGHT, INTENTION, AND LANGUAGE: DIFFERENCES OF CATEGORY

We have seen that in Wittgenstein's early philosophy the concept of thought was assimilated to the concept of language: thinking is a kind of language. In his later philosophy the concept of thinking is recognised to belong to a different category from that of language:

> It isn't true that thinking is a kind of speaking, as I once said. The concept 'thinking' is *categorically* different from the concept 'speaking'.[48]

'Talking' (whether out loud or silently) and 'thinking' are not concepts of the same kind; even though they are in closest connexion.[49]

If the two concepts were of the same kind, it would be possible for the process of thinking a thought to accompany the utterance of a sentence (out loud or silently), and perhaps it would be necessary for it to do so if the utterance of the sentence were to be the expression of a thought. Moreover, the lightning-like thought that flashes through one's mind would need to be a speeded up inner analogue of the outward expression of thought.[50] But 'thinking a thought' is not the name of a *process* of any kind (and so it is not an experience or state of consciousness) and the concepts of thinking a thought and uttering a sentence are therefore radically different from each other.[51] A thought lacks duration: it is neither a uniform state lasting from one point in time to another nor a series of distinguishable phases of a process occurring in a segment of time. Hence, thinking a thought cannot accompany a spoken sentence and the 'process' of thinking cannot occur in an accelerated form in lightning-like thought. And hence also the concepts of thinking and intention (in one sense) are alike:

> The intention *with which* one acts does not 'accompany' the action any more than the thought 'accompanies' speech. Thought and intention are neither 'articulated' nor 'non-articulated'; to be compared neither with a single note which sounds during the acting or speaking, nor with a tune.[52]

For these reasons, a thought and an intention in action 'consist of nothing'.[53] Nevertheless, an intention in action is not a thought: an intention can be present in my action on an occasion when I do not have a thought with the thought-content of the intention, as when I mean you to write one number after another when I ask you to develop a series in accordance with a formula, but without my having thought of what you should do at that point.[54]

It is consistent with Wittgenstein's approach to philosophy that his investigation of the concepts of thought and intention should go only as far as he thought was necessary to undermine seductive misconceptions of the concepts. His fundamental insight is the realisation that it does not follow from a specification of the non-representational nature of any item that is a representation that it is a representation, and, in particular, that it is a representation of whatever in fact it is a representation of. So a non-semantic specification of the sounds I utter does not entail a semantic characterisation of them. And this point holds for imagery and silent speech just as much as for pictures and speech proper. Hence it is not the intrinsic, non-representational nature of anything that happens when I think a thought or intend something a certain way that determines what I think or intend. And hence it is not the intrinsic, non-representational nature of anything that happens to my state of consciousness that determines what, if anything, I think or intend at that time. Now by far the major part of Wittgenstein's examination of the concepts of thought and intention is taken up with multifarious variations on this theme, and his positive suggestions, which occupy little space, are not worked out in detail. I have tried to indicate what these suggestions are, but it is clear that much work remains to be done if a thorough understanding of the concepts of thought and intention is to be obtained.

VII

FEELINGS, EMOTIONS
AND THE BODY

CONCEPTS OF FEELING

An everyday psychological concept can be of such an indefinite nature, accommodating phenomena of radically different kinds, that its content is too bare to sustain interest in abstraction from a specific application of the concept. A prime example is the concept of a feeling. Consider the variety of things I might feel: a pain in my ankle, fear, joy or depression, conviction, dependency, awkwardness, energy or tiredness, dizziness, the position or movement of my arm, and the explicitly propositional feelings that something is about to happen or that I have been in just the same situation before or that my surroundings are unreal. Many of these so-called feelings are examined by Wittgenstein and in each case his investigation is conceptual or grammatical. His interest is the determination of the psychological category to which the feeling should be assigned.[1] Perhaps the two best models of Wittgenstein's method are his treatment of the concept of our immediate feeling of the position and movement of our limbs – our feeling how a limb is disposed or moving without feeling the limb with another part of the body – and his treatment of the topic of the emotions. These two examples each involve the idea of a feeling, although they involve it in different ways and the feelings fall into different psychological categories. It is true that an emotion need not be felt when it occurs. But emotions often are and always can be felt, and to each emotion there is a corresponding emotional feeling – a feeling of anger, jealousy, embarrassment, remorse, or whatever. The reason for Wittgenstein's special interest in these two different kinds of feeling is his belief that there is a strong tendency to reduce each feeling to the favoured paradigm of a feeling, a bodily sensation. I begin with the simpler of the two cases.[2]

AWARENESS OF BODILY POSITION AND MOVEMENT

It is clear that we possess the capacity – a capacity that is integral to intentional action – to be aware of our bodily posture and movements without making use of our eyes or feeling one part of our body with another part. But the nature of this direct awareness is problematic.[3] For if we are asked how we know the position or movement of a part of our body, the natural response is to say that we *feel* it. Yet it is unclear how this reference to a feeling is to be understood. What kind of concept is the concept of feeling my left arm to be behind my back or my head to be nodding up and down?

Wittgenstein's leading idea is that we do not judge the position and movement of our limbs by the feelings that these positions and movements give us.[4] Although we can feel the position and movement of a limb, the *bodily sensations* caused by the limb's being in that position or making that movement do not tell us what the position or movement is.[5]

In explanation and defence of this thesis Wittgenstein advances a number of considerations about the existence and nature of the bodily sensations caused by the position or movement of a limb and their relation to my direct awareness of the limb's position or movement. In the first place, it is normally the case that the sensations in the part of the body whose position or movement I have direct awareness of are insufficient to provide me with the knowledge I possess. If I follow Wittgenstein's example and let one of my index fingers make a small pendulum movement, I am likely to find that I feel only a slight tension in the tip of the finger, and the exact knowledge of the movement cannot be read off this bodily sensation.[6] Or if my finger is bent and I am directly aware of this, I may be unaware of any sensation in the finger that I would not feel if the finger were straight, and there may be no sensation missing that would be present if the finger were not

147

bent.[7] Secondly, whatever sensations I may feel when I attend to
my posture or bodily movement, there is no ground for assuming
that I feel these sensations when my attention is otherwise
engaged.[8] Nevertheless, I am not unaware of the position and
motion of my body when I am not concentrating upon it. Thirdly,
the fact that my finger would feel different if it were anaesthetized does not imply that I do feel some sensation in it when
normally I move it; for to say that I felt nothing when moving the
finger in a certain way on a particular occasion is not to say that it
felt as if there were no sensation in it.[9] Furthermore, if it is true
that I lose my direct awareness of the position and movement of
a limb when it is anaesthetized, it does not follow that normally I
know of its position and movement by means of a sensation that
is distinctive of that position or movement.[10] Finally, there is no
reason to suppose that any sensation I experience on a particular
occasion when a limb is in a certain position or is moving in a
certain manner is experienced whenever I am aware of the limb's
being in that position or moving in that way. For example, I am
unlikely to feel the same sensation in moving a limb if the
movement is very painful or if I am exceptionally tired, and yet
my direct awareness of its movement does not then desert me.[11]

It would be possible for someone to reply to these observations
with the assertion that his own case is different and that he *does*
judge the kind and magnitude of the movement of a limb by a
type of sensation that varies in strength or quality with difference
of movements. Wittgenstein concedes such a possibility.[12] The
issue that concerns him is the nature of the requirement that must
be satisfied if it is to be true that someone does judge the position
or movement of his limbs by the kind of sensation produced by
that position or movement. One condition he insists upon is that
it must be possible to specify the nature of the sensation that
supposedly informs the person of his bodily attitude or movement
independently of a specification of the attitude or movement: if it
does not possess an independent intrinsic nature, the person does
not judge the position or motion of his body by the sensation.[13]
And his fundamental point is that it would be mistaken to
maintain that this requirement must be satisfied by our immediate awareness of the position and movement of our limbs. Just as
it would be wrong to insist that when I experience a pain in my
body I must experience both pain and a sign which indicates

where the pain is (a local sign);[14] or when I remember a past event there must be some characteristic of my image which indicates the temporal position of the event (a temporal sign);[15] so it would be wrong to insist that when I am directly aware of the position or movement of a limb I must experience a sensation which provides me with the information. In each case the relevant concept does not impose this requirement.

THE FEELING OF MOTION AND POSITION

Let us now consider the *feeling* of motion and position. We have in effect seen that we should distinguish between the feeling that I am raising my arm and the sensations that occur in my arm when I raise it. Suppose that I feel such-and-such sensations when I raise my arm. It is an empirical proposition that I feel those (or any other) sensations when I raise my arm. But it is not an empirical proposition that the feeling I get when I raise my arm – my feeling the movement of my arm – is the feeling that I am raising my arm.[16] To find out what sensations occur in my arm when I raise it I must conduct the experiment of raising my arm and set myself to observe what sensations, if any, this brings about in it; and this experiment will show me only the sensations I experience on that occasion, not the sensations I experience whenever I raise my arm. But no experiment is even relevant to determining which feeling is the feeling of my raising my arm.

There is a positive and a negative side to Wittgenstein's account of the concept of my feeling my bodily posture and the movement of my limbs. The negative aspect consists in the denial that the feeling is in the category of sensation, and in particular of bodily sensation. Let us understand by a bodily sensation a psychological occurrence that is comparable to bodily pain in that it possesses (i) intensity, (ii) quality, (iii) genuine duration, and (iv) location.[17] Then the feeling of position and motion fails to qualify as a bodily sensation on all four counts. Although the sensations that occur in my arm when it is in a particular position or when I move it may be stronger or weaker, my feeling of its position or movement is not subject to degrees.[18] Neither does it possess a quality comparable to timbre or hue, which allows of blends or mixtures of different instances of the quality and which is such that one instance can be more or less like another instance.[19] In consequence, there is a lack of adjectives comparable to colour terms or words for timbre by the use of which I can describe the nature of the feeling I have when I feel my arm to be behind my back. And because the feeling of position lacks both intensity and quality, it does not possess the same kind of duration as a sensation of sound or colour: there is no possibility of correlating variations in its intrinsic nature with variations in sound or colour.[20] It is for these reasons that if we mistakenly conceive of our direct awareness of our posture as a sensation,[21] we will be liable to think of it as having no content or subjective aspect.[22] Finally, the feeling of position does not itself possess a position in the body: when I feel a pain I feel it in a part of my body, but when I feel my arm to be behind my back I do not feel this feeling to be in my arm. It follows that if we conceive of our direct awareness of the position of a limb as a kind of bodily sensation, we will experience the inclination to attribute a position to the feeling of position:

I feel my arm and, oddly, I should like to say: I feel it in a particular position in space: as if, that is, my bodily feeling were distributed in a space in the shape of an arm, so that in order to represent the matter, I would have to represent the arm, say in plaster, in the right position. It is odd. My lower arm is now lying horizontally and I should like to say I feel that; but not as if I had a feeling that always goes with this position (as one would feel ischaemia or congestion) – rather as if the 'bodily feeling' of the arm were arranged or distributed horizontally, as, e.g., a film of damp or of fine dust on the surface of my arm is distributed like that in space. So it isn't really as if I felt the position of my arm, but rather as if I felt my *arm*, and the feeling had such and such a *position*. But that only means: I simply *know* how it is lying – without knowing it *because* . . . . As I also know where I feel pain – but don't know it *because* . . . .[23]

The moral that Wittgenstein draws at the end of these remarks is the one we have already recognised: it is misguided to hypostatise a kinaesthetic sensation, some characteristic of which provides me with the information I possess about the position and movement of my limbs.

Wittgenstein's positive suggestion is that my feeling of position or movement is nothing other than my immediate conviction that a part of my body is in a certain position or is moving in a certain manner. So he suggests that rather than recognising a series of sensations as that which is characteristic of moving my arm up and down, and thereby knowing how I am moving it, my certainty that I am moving it in this way is constitutive of my *feeling* that this is how I am moving it.[24] The fact of the matter is that I know of the position of my limbs and their movements without observation, and there is nothing more to the concept of being able to feel where they are or how they are moving than the idea of this direct awareness. The only intrinsic property of the feeling that my hand is behind my back is that which it has in virtue of its representational content.

A SKETCH OF THE CONCEPT OF THE EMOTIONS

We can now turn to the topic of the emotions.[25] The main lines of Wittgenstein's investigation of the concept of emotion are clear: he elucidates the concept by reference to a small number of features that either make the category of emotion comparable with or distinguish it from other psychological categories; he indicates an important distinction within the class of emotions; and his principal target is the James–Lange theory of the emotions, which represents an emotion, or the experience of feeling the emotion, as being composed of a set of bodily sensations.

Let us consider an emotion not in the dispositional, but in the episodic sense: the sense in which I might feel acute fear on some occasion, rather than the sense in which I might have a 'chronic' fear of someone.[26] Then the brief outline of Wittgenstein's account can be filled in as follows. He identifies one feature that is not only common to the emotions, but which the class of emotions shares with the class of sensations: the members of each class possess 'genuine duration': they may run on uniformly or non-uniformly.[27] He specifies one feature that distinguishes the emotions from *bodily* sensations: an emotion has no place: it is neither localized nor diffuse.[28] Two additional features are claimed to distinguish the emotions from the more inclusive category of sensation: (i) the emotions, unlike sensations, do not give us any information about the external world,[29] and (ii) the emotions, unlike sensations, can 'colour' thoughts.[30] And the emotions are united not only by the possession of genuine duration and the capacity to colour thoughts, the lack of a place in the body and the absence of information about the external world, but also by the fact that each emotion has a characteristic expression in the body or behaviour, and hence also characteristic bodily sensations.[31] Finally, within the class of emotions, 'directed emotions' can be distinguished from 'undirected emotions'.[32]

DIRECTED AND UNDIRECTED EMOTIONS

I begin with the distinction between directed and undirected emotions. Now Wittgenstein does not make it clear whether to each kind of directed emotion there is a corresponding kind of undirected emotion, and, if not, what explains this fact; but his view appears to be that certain kinds of emotion are always directed emotions, whereas other kinds of emotion are sometimes undirected. A directed emotion is one that has an object, an undirected emotion is one that does not. But what is it for an emotion to be directed towards an object? Although Wittgenstein illustrates the concept of a directed emotion, he does little to explicate it. The basic idea is that if fear is fear *at* something or joy is joy *over* something then the emotion is directed and the something at which the emotion is directed or about which it is concerned is the object of the emotion. If, on the contrary, someone experiences an emotion which is not *at*, *over* (*in*, *that*, etc.) something, the emotion is undirected and it lacks an object. It is of course a commonplace that there are apparently objectless states of emotion, in which someone is dejected, anxious, or euphoric without there being any specific thing or fact that he recognises as, or that seems to be, the target[33] of his emotion: there are 'free-floating' episodes of emotion. But without an elucidation of the concept of a directed emotion (alternatively, the concept of an emotion's object) it remains unclear whether this is merely appearance and the object of the emotion is in these cases hidden in some way that normally it is not.

Wittgenstein's handling of the distinction between a directed and an undirected emotion has a negative and a positive side. On the one hand, he asserts that if an emotion is directed towards something, 'this something is the object, not the cause of the emotion'. On the other hand, he claims that 'the language-game "I am afraid" already contains the object'.[34]

Let us take the negative aspect first. Wittgenstein's assertion that the target of an emotion is its object, not its cause, is not intended to imply that the object of an emotion cannot also be its cause. He himself remarks that the typical causes of depression, sorrow, and joy are also their objects.[35] His fundamental point is that the concept of the object of an emotion is not the concept of its cause. He also appears to believe that the concept of a directed emotion cannot be analysed in causal terms.[36] He certainly repudiates the idea that the relation between my fear and you when my fear is directed at you is just the relation between my pain and the cause of the pain. And he seems also to reject the proposal that the idea of a directed emotion should be analysed causally in terms of the idea of the corresponding undirected emotion, as it were, and the subject's knowledge of the cause of this emotion. Following Wittgenstein's suggestion that undirected fear might be called 'anxiety',[37] this rejected analysis represents a case in which I feel afraid of John as differing from one in which I feel anxious only in the respect that in the former case I know (or perhaps merely believe) that John is the cause of my emotion. But it is obvious that my knowledge that something is the cause or a cause of my fear, depression, sorrow or joy is insufficient for my emotion to be directed towards that thing: a known cause of my emotion is not thereby what my emotion is *at*, *over*, *in*, or *about*, or in some other way its target. Wittgenstein would therefore be right to reject this proposal.

The positive side of Wittgenstein's account of the concept of a directed emotion consists of the obscurely formulated idea that 'the language-game "I am afraid" already contains the object'. What this appears to mean is that I do not need to carry out any kind of causal investigation to determine whose death I am grieving over or whether my fear is directed at Jack or at Jill, for if I have mastered our language I have learnt when to utter the verbal expression of a directed emotion, and this indicates the object or state of affairs towards which the emotion is directed. The idea would be that in certain circumstances – ones in which someone or something is behaving towards me in a threatening manner and I react with signs of fear – I have been taught to say 'I am afraid of . . .', where '. . .' designates the threatening object, and my mastery of this form of words carries with it the authority to specify, and also to reject a suggested specification of, the object of the emotion. Accordingly, given that I have mastered this segment of the language, if I feel an emotion but recognise nothing as the object of my emotion, the emotion lacks an object and is therefore undirected.

Two things are clear about such an account. The first is that it stands in need of considerable elaboration if it is to be at all plausible. Apart from any other considerations, it appears to presuppose an unexplained notion of the directedness of an emotion, as is particularly evident in the case of the directed emotions of languageless creatures.[38] The second is that this style of account is not only consonant with Wittgenstein's elucidation of the idea of the thought-content of psychological states, but is forced upon him in virtue of the restricted way in which he understands the philosophy of psychology as a purely descriptive discipline concerned only with the so-called grammar of psychological words.

THE EMOTIONAL COLOURING OF THOUGHTS

I now turn to one of the features that Wittgenstein uses to differentiate the emotions from sensations: emotions, unlike sensations, can 'colour' thoughts: thoughts can be joyful, angry, fearful, hopeful, loathsome, regretful or enchanting, but not toothache-ish.[39] Wittgenstein offers little in explanation of this idea. An identification of the idea of a thought's being coloured by an emotion with the idea of the thought's causing the emotion might appear to be suggested by certain remarks in *Zettel*:

> Thoughts may be fearful, hopeful, joyful, angry, etc. Emotions are expressed in thoughts. A man talks angrily, timidly, sadly, joyfully etc., not lumbagoishly.

154

A thought rouses emotions in me (fear, sorrow etc) not bodily pain.[40]

But just as it would be mistaken to identify the concept of an emotion's being directed to an object with the concept of the emotion's being caused by the object, so it would be mistaken to identify the concept of a thought's being coloured by an emotion with the concept of the thought's causing the emotion. In fact, the concept of a directed emotion is included in the concept of a thought that is coloured with emotion. For a regretful, sad or angry thought is not simply one that causes me to experience regret, sadness or anger, but one I think *with* that emotion; and to think a thought with regret, sadness or anger is to experience an emotion that is directed towards some constituent of the content of the thought.

This interpretation of the idea of a thought's being coloured by an emotion is confirmed if we briefly consider Wittgenstein's treatment of the concept of pleasure. His principal target is the idea that pleasure is a sensation, but his remarks have a wider reference:

> Someone who asks whether pleasure is a sensation probably does not distinguish between ground and cause, for otherwise it would occur to him that one has pleasure *in something*, which does not mean that this something causes a sensation in us.[41]

> A smell may be extremely pleasant. Is what is pleasant about it only a sensation? In that case the sensation of pleasantness would accompany the smell. But how would it *relate to the smell*?[42]

Now a pleasant thought is one that I think with pleasure, and it is just as much a misrepresentation to conceive of my pleasure as something I experience and that merely accompanies my thought as it is to conceive of the pleasure of a pleasant smell as an accompaniment of the smell. No matter what my pleasure might be taken to be, in each case the problem of how it is related to what it accompanies (and is caused by) would arise, for no combination of a thought or smell and an accompanying effect would be sufficient for the thought or smell to be experienced *as* pleasant.

155

The similarity between Wittgenstein's concern with the concept of pleasure and his understanding of the idea of the emotional colouring of a thought is apparent in such remarks as these:

> If I say 'Every time I thought about it I was afraid' – did fear *accompany* my thoughts? – How is one to conceive of separating what does the accompanying from what is accompanied? We could ask: How does fear pervade a thought? For the former does not seem to be merely concurrent with the latter . . .
> One also says: 'Thinking about it takes my breath away', and means not only that as a matter of experience this or that sensation or reaction accompanies this thought.
> To the utterance: 'I can't think of it without fear' one replies: 'There's no reason for fear, for . . . .' That is at any rate one way of dismissing fear. Contrast with pain.[43]

It is therefore clear that Wittgenstein rejects the idea that fear is merely caused by and concurrent with a thought it colours, and his positive suggestion seems to be that the thought contains or implies the reason or ground of fear, so that the fear is amenable or vulnerable to reason. But this suggestion is undeveloped, and Wittgenstein's explication of the concept of emotion does not include sufficient materials to explain why the emotions can be responsive to reason.

EMOTIONS AND INFORMATION ABOUT THE EXTERNAL WORLD

Perhaps it is the susceptibility of an emotion to reason that explains the second feature that Wittgenstein uses to distinguish the emotions from sensations: the emotions, unlike sensations, do not give us any information about the external world. We have seen that Wittgenstein makes use of the idea that an item of a certain psychological kind does not provide us with information about the external world both in his account of the concept of seeing an aspect and in that of visualising, and in each case the reason he gives for saying that an item of that category does not tell us about the external world is that such an item is 'subject to the will'.[44] We have also seen that there is some difficulty in understanding and assessing the exact force of the idea that a psychological phenomenon is subject to the will. Since Wittgenstein does not offer any elucidation of his characterisation of the grammar of words for emotions by reference to the proposition that the emotions do not give us any information about the external world, any interpretation must be purely speculative. However, it would at least be consistent both with Wittgenstein's remarks about subjection to the will and with his remarks about the emotions, including the manner in which they can colour a thought, to interpret his grammatical characterisation in the following way. The emotions do not give us any information about the external world – this is the interpretation – insofar as it makes sense to say to someone who is experiencing an emotion, 'Don't feel afraid, angry, sad, depressed, jealous (or whatever), because . . .', where '. . .' specifies a reason for the person not to feel the emotion he is undergoing. But this suggestion would need to be founded in an account of the relation between thought and the nature of the emotions of a kind that Wittgenstein does not provide.

WILLIAM JAMES'S THEORY OF THE EMOTIONS

According to Wittgenstein, the specific mark that distinguishes the emotions from bodily sensations is that whereas a bodily sensation has a location in the body, an emotion has no place: it is neither localized nor diffused throughout the body. Hence an emotion is neither a single bodily sensation nor a mass of sensations variously localized in the body. And this is true not because, or not solely in virtue of the fact, that there is *more* to any emotion than whatever bodily sensations may be experienced when the emotion is felt. Wittgenstein's point is the stronger claim that my *feeling* of anger, fear or sadness cannot be identified with any bodily sensations I may feel at the time. Such sensations are only *accompaniments* of my feeling of anger, fear or sadness. Since Wittgenstein's position conflicts with the James–Lange theory of the emotions, against which his remark that emotions are not diffuse is specifically directed, it will be helpful to consider the theory in the form with which Wittgenstein

157

was familiar, as elaborated by William James in *The Principles of Psychology.*[45]

James put forward the theory that whenever I experience emotion, my emotion just is the feeling of those bodily changes that are reflex effects of my awareness (whether in perception or thought) of the object of my emotion. It follows that if I were not to experience any bodily sensations as a result of my awareness of an object, my awareness would be purely cognitive or intellectual, so that I would not *feel* angry when insulted or afraid when in danger: I would merely recognise the nature of the situation and judge what it would be best or appropriate for me to do. James did not believe that whenever I feel a certain emotion (fear, say) I must or do experience the same bodily sensations as anyone else experiences when undergoing that emotion; and he also did not believe that whenever I feel the same kind of emotion I must or do experience the same bodily sensations. His thesis that the feeling I have when I feel angry, afraid, or sad is identical with the complex of sensations aroused by the bodily manifestations of the emotion allows that my feelings of anger, fear, or sadness vary from occasion to occasion, as do those of other people. The claim is that on each occasion the feeling is identical with the sensations caused by whatever bodily changes are produced on that occasion by my awareness of the emotion's object.

James did not advance his theory as a proposition that was 'in the nature of things' necessary.[46] He believed, however, that the theory must hold for human beings, so that 'a purely disembodied human emotion is a nonentity'.[47] In defence of the theory he made this claim:

> every one of the bodily changes, whatsoever it be, is FELT, acutely or obscurely, the moment it occurs.[48]

And he identified the following assertion as the 'vital point' of his theory:

> If we fancy some strong emotion, and then try to abstract from our consciousness of it all the feelings of its bodily symptoms, we find we have nothing left behind, no 'mind-stuff' out of which the emotion can be constituted.[49]

158

Now at the time he dictated the *Brown Book* Wittgenstein was sympathetic to James's theory and he embraced the view that the feeling of anger or sadness is partly composed of bodily feelings:

> Remember at this point that the personal experiences of any emotion must in part be strictly localized experiences; for if I frown in anger I feel the muscular tension of the frown in my forehead, and if I weep, the sensations around my eyes are obviously part, and an important part, of what I feel. This is, I think, what William James meant when he said that a man doesn't cry because he is sad but that he is sad because he cries.[50]

But Wittgenstein later rejected each of the elements of James's position that I have picked out, and also a further element that I have not yet introduced.

Let us begin with James's claim that each bodily change that takes place when an emotion is experienced is itself felt. Here is Wittgenstein's denial of this thesis:

> There is no ground for assuming that a man feels the facial movements that go with his expression, for example, or the alterations in his breathing that are characteristic of some emotion. Even if he feels them as soon as his attention is directed towards them.[51]

This does no more than oppose James's claim with a counter-assertion, and the indefiniteness of the concept of feeling precludes a simple resolution of the issue. But if we understand the concept in such a way that a person must be conscious or aware of anything he feels, the point is incontrovertible and is economically expressed in this passage:

> If someone imitates grief for himself in his study, he will indeed readily be conscious of the tensions in his face. But really grieve, or follow a sorrowful action in a film, and ask yourself if you were conscious of your face.[52]

This effects the introduction of the further aspect of James's theory with which Wittgenstein took issue. According to the theory, an emotion is the bodily sensations of its so-called manifestations. It can therefore be at least partially reproduced by intentionally assuming its characteristic bodily expression – its normal facial expression, for example. But, as James emphasizes,[53] many of the manifestations of an emotion are in parts of the body over which we have no voluntary control, and it is therefore unlikely that the adoption of the bodily attitude characteristic of an emotion will induce the emotion itself. Accordingly:

> the attempt to imitate an emotion in the absence of its normal instigating cause is apt to be rather 'hollow'.[54]

Nevertheless, James maintained that his theory is corroborated by the fact that an emotion, or at least some pale version of it, is liable to be experienced if its outward appearance is mimicked. As we have seen, Wittgenstein concedes that if I imitate the bodily expression of an emotion and concentrate my attention upon my body as I do so, I will experience feelings in my body at those parts which I have made assume the form of the expression of the emotion. He also allows that mimicry of the bodily attitude expressive of an emotion might be conducive to a change in my emotional condition from a state of depression, say, to one of cheerfulness.[55] But it does not follow that my feeling of fear, joy or sadness is partly or wholly composed of bodily sensations.

Wittgenstein's principal argument against the identification of my feeling of fear or joy with the bodily sensations I experience when I deliberately adopt the bodily attitude characteristic of the emotion and attend to how my body feels – the argument applies in the first instance and with equal, if not greater, force to the identification of an emotional feeling with the sensations experienced in a full-blooded case of emotion – is that the proposed identification violates Leibniz's Law. For the experience of the emotion possesses a property that the sensations lack. My fear is a distressing, perhaps a horrible, experience and my joy is rewarding, but my bodily sensations of fear will usually be easy to endure and are unlikely to be horrible and those of joy unlikely to be rewarding:

> 'Horrible fear': is it the *sensations* that are so horrible?[56]

> Is it so disagreeable, so sad, to draw down the corners of one's mouth, and so pleasant to pull them up? What is it that is so frightful about fear? The trembling, the quick breathing, the feeling in the facial muscles? When you say: 'This fear, this uncertainty, is frightful!' – might you go on 'If only I didn't

have this feeling in my stomach!'? When anxiety is frightful, and when in anxiety I am conscious of my breathing and of a tension in the muscles of my face – does that mean that I find *these feelings* frightful? Might they not even signify an alleviation?[57]

Hence the supposition that if I make a joyful face my state of depression will be lightened to some extent and I will have a feeling of joy does not imply that my feelings of depression and joy are composed of bodily sensations. For the reason that I feel better will not be that I have replaced a set of unpleasant bodily sensations with a set of pleasant ones:

> Does one say: 'Now I feel much better: the feeling in my facial muscles and round about the corners of my mouth is good'? And why does that sound laughable, except, say, when one had felt pain in these parts before?[58]

Now it is easy to extend Wittgenstein's observations to cover a wide range of emotions. Thus it is not the bodily sensations I experience when I feel pride or remorse that makes the feeling of pride rewarding or satisfying and the feeling of remorse painful or distressing. But if this style of argument is to yield the conclusion that nobody's emotional feeling is ever identical with his concurrent bodily sensations, it must be true both that each episode of emotion is in some way pleasurable or unpleasurable and that the bodily sensations produced by awareness of the object of an emotion are never pleasurable or unpleasurable in the same manner as the emotion. There is, however, a closely-related style of argument that requires only the first of these two propositions to be true. For even if on some occasion my bodily sensations of the manifestations of my emotion possess the same hedonic quality as my feeling of the emotion, my feeling will not be identical with these bodily sensations unless what I find pleasurable or unpleasurable *in feeling the emotion* is this compound of bodily sensations. But at least in the case of directed emotions this condition will not be satisfied. For the delight or distress that is intrinsic to my experience of the emotion is not delight *in* or distress *at* the bodily sensations I experience: it is directed towards the object of my emotion. It is clear that this consideration was for Wittgenstein an additional

161

reason for resisting the identification of a person's feeling of an emotion with any concurrent bodily sensations he might experience, and it is perhaps this reason that is operative when he considers a situation in which someone's emotion *would* have a similar hedonic quality to that of his bodily sensation:

> If there were people who felt a stabbing pain in their left side in those cases where we express misgivings with feelings of anxiety – would this stabbing sensation take the place with them of our feeling of fear? – So if we observed these people and noticed them wincing and holding their left side every time they expressed a misgiving, i.e., said something which for us at any rate would be a misgiving – would we say: These people sense their fear as a stabbing pain? Clearly not.[59]

Moreover, even if some form of pleasure or pain is not intrinsic to each occurrence of emotion, the intentionality of an emotional feeling rules out its identification with any bodily sensations.

The final element of James's account that Wittgenstein rejects is the so-called vital point of the theory, the imaginability claim. It is clear that Wittgenstein must regard James's claim as unwarranted. For, as we have seen, Wittgenstein believes that I can experience an emotion without feeling the changes in my body in which the emotion is manifested. Hence, if what is conceptually possible is thereby imaginable, it cannot be impossible to imagine myself undergoing an emotion without any contemporaneous awareness of feelings of its bodily symptoms. James's confidence in his imaginability claim perhaps derived from a conflation of these two distinct propositions:

(i) It is not possible for me to imagine myself both experiencing an emotion and simultaneously, with my attention directed towards the changes taking place in my body, feeling nothing (i.e., being anaesthetic),

and

(ii) It is not possible for me to imagine myself experiencing an emotion without being simultaneously aware of bodily sensations induced by the manifestations of the emotion in my body.

162

Wittgenstein argues against James's imaginability claim in a different way from this by connecting it with the idea of mimicry:

> James says it is impossible to imagine an emotion or a mood without the corresponding bodily sensations (of which it is composed). If you imagine the latter absent then you can see that you are thereby abolishing the very existence of the emotion. This might happen in the following way: I imagine myself sorrowing, and now in the imagination I try to picture and feel myself rejoicing at the same time. To do that I might take a deep breath and imitate a beaming face. And now indeed I have trouble forming an image of sorrow; for forming an image of it would mean play-acting it. But it does not follow from this that our bodily feeling at that point is sorrow, or even something like it.[60]

But there is some uncertainty, or at least obscurity, in Wittgenstein's argument. His suggestion appears to be that there is indeed a difficulty in carrying out James's project if it is construed as requiring me to assume simultaneously the bodily expressions of two emotions that have different and incompatible expressions in the body. But there is little appeal to the idea that James's claim derives its plausibility from a surreptitious exploitation of this impossibility. A better suggestion, which is perhaps what Wittgenstein intended, would be that I will find it difficult to imagine an emotion remaining when I subtract from its imaginative realisation the corresponding bodily sensations, if I attempt to do this by adopting and feeling the bodily expression of one emotion while imagining myself to feel an emotion with an incompatible bodily expression. But although this is a better suggestion, in fact there is no reason to try to refute James's suggestion in this exceptionally strong manner, by the imaginative addition of the sensations and bodily expression characteristic of one emotion to the experience of another. It is sufficient to imagine the experience of an emotion in abstraction from the sensations characteristic of the emotion itself. And this is not a difficult task.

THE EMOTIONS AND INTROSPECTION

As I have indicated, James did not maintain that his identification of each episode of emotion with an experience of bodily sensations was 'in the nature of things' necessary. But the object of Wittgenstein's investigation is the *concept* of emotion and he opposes James's identification on the ground that it does not provide a correct answer to the question, 'What is it for someone to feel an emotion?', where this asks for an elucidation of the concept of someone's feeling an emotion.[61] James's theory of the emotions assigns emotion to the wrong psychological category. The reason for Wittgenstein's special interest in James's theory and the explanation of what might in some ways seem to be Wittgenstein's unfair criticism of it is that Wittgenstein considered the attractiveness of the theory to derive from a prevalent but mistaken method for gaining insight into the essence of a psychological kind. At the heart of Wittgenstein's philosophy of psychology is his rejection of introspection as a means of obtaining information about everyday psychological concepts, and it is because he sees the charm of James's theory as stemming from its appeal to introspection that he is particularly concerned to combat it.[62] His fundamental objection to James's hypothesis that feeling an emotion consists in the experience of a complex of bodily sensations is that the determination of the truth of the hypothesis in one's own case would require one to attend to oneself to see what happens when one feels an emotion, and for that reason the hypothesis cannot capture the content of what one means when one attributes an emotion to oneself:

> Something that could only be established by an act of *looking* – that's at any rate not what you meant.
> For 'sorrow', 'joy' etc. just are not used like that.[63]

Furthermore, it is Wittgenstein's opposition to the idea that an appropriate way to determine what a psychological word means is to attend to what happens in or to ourselves when the word applies to us that lies behind his rejection of James's view that the bodily manifestations of an emotion are always felt ('acutely or obscurely').[64] Moreover, this opposition also explains his concern to make the point, in connection with James's appeal to

164

what someone will feel if he imitates the bodily attitude expressive of an emotion, that it is not an *a priori* or necessary truth that whoever imitates or play-acts joy or fear will feel the emotion.[65] And, finally, the force of Wittgenstein's most dramatic rejection of the idea that an emotion is a composition of bodily sensations (or anything else) is the implication that introspection is an inappropriate method for the investigation of the nature of an emotion:

> 'But "joy" surely designates an inward thing.' No. 'Joy' designates nothing at all. Neither any inward nor any outward thing'.[66]

The repudiation of the model of 'object and designation' for everyday psychological words – the denial that the picture of the inner process provides a correct representation of the grammar of such words – is not the only reason for Wittgenstein's hostility to the use of introspection in the philosophy of psychology. But it is its ultimate foundation.

LIST OF ABBREVIATIONS

AWL   Ambrose, A. (ed.) (1979) *Wittgenstein's Lectures, Cambridge 1932–1935*, from the notes of A. Ambrose and M. MacDonald, Oxford: Basil Blackwell.

BB   Wittgenstein, L. (1960) *The Blue and Brown Books*, Oxford: Basil Blackwell.

LA   Barrett, C. (ed.) (1966) *Lectures and Conversations on Aesthetics, Psychology and Religious Belief*, compiled from the notes taken by Y. Smith, R. Rhees, and J. Taylor, Oxford: Basil Blackwell.

LFM   Diamond, C. (ed.) (1976) *Wittgenstein's Lectures on the Foundations of Mathematics, Cambridge 1939*, from the notes of R. G. Bosanquet, N. Malcolm, R. Rhees, and Y. Smithies, Sussex: Harvester Press.

LPE   Rhees, R. (ed.) 'Wittgenstein's Notes for Lectures on "Private Experience" and "Sense Data"', *The Philosophical Review* vol. LXXVII, no. 3, July 1968.

LW   Wittgenstein, L. (1982) *Last Writings on the Philosophy of Psychology*, vol. I, C. G. Luckhardt and M. A. E. Aue (trs.), G. H. von Wright and H. Nyman (eds), Oxford: Basil Blackwell.

LWL   Lee, D. (ed.) (1982) *Wittgenstein's Lectures, Cambridge 1930–1932*, from the notes of J. King and D. Lee, Oxford: Basil Blackwell.

LWM   Malcolm, N. (1959) *Ludwig Wittgenstein, A Memoir*, with a biographical sketch by G. H. von Wright, London: Oxford University Press.

M   Moore, G. E. (1959) 'Wittgenstein's Lectures in 1930–33', *Philosophical Papers*, London: George Allen & Unwin.

NB   Wittgenstein, L. (1979) *Notebooks 1914–1916*, second edition,

List of abbreviations

G. E. M. Anscombe (tr.) G. H. von Wright and G. E. M.
Anscombe (eds), Oxford: Basil Blackwell.

OC   Wittgenstein, L. (1969) *On Certainty*, D. Paul and G. E. M.
Anscombe (trs), G. E. M. Anscombe and G. H. von Wright
(eds), Oxford: Basil Blackwell.

PG   Wittgenstein, L. (1974) *Philosophical Grammar*, A. Kenny
(tr.), R. Rhees (ed.), Oxford: Basil Blackwell.

PI   Wittgenstein, L. (1958) *Philosophical Investigations*, second
edition, G. E. M. Anscombe (tr.), G. E. M. Anscombe and
R. Rhees (eds), Oxford: Basil Blackwell.

PR   Wittgenstein, L. (1975) *Philosophical Remarks*, R. Hargreaves
and R. White (trs), R. Rhees (ed.), Oxford: Basil Blackwell.

RFM   Wittgenstein, L. (1978) *Remarks on the Foundations of
Mathematics*, third edn, G. E. M. Anscombe (tr.), G. H. von
Wright, R. Rhees, and G. E. M. Anscombe (eds), Oxford:
Basil Blackwell.

ROC   Wittgenstein, L. (1977) *Remarks on Colour*, L. L. McAlister
and M. Schättle (trs), G. E. M. Anscombe (ed.), Oxford: Basil
Blackwell.

RPPI,   Wittgenstein, L. (1980) *Remarks on the Philosophy of
RPPII   Psychology*, vol. I, G. E. M. Anscombe (tr.), G. E. M.
Anscombe and G. H. von Wright (eds); vol. II, C. G. Luck-
hardt and M. A. E. Aue (trs), G. H. von Wright and
H. Nyman (eds), Oxford: Basil Blackwell.

TLP   Wittgenstein, L. (1961) *Tractatus Logico-Philosophicus*,
D. F. Pears and B. F. McGuinness (trs), London: Routledge &
Kegan Paul.

Z   Wittgenstein, L. (1981) *Zettel*, second edition, G. E. M.
Anscombe (tr.), G. E. M. Anscombe and G. H. von Wright
(eds), Oxford: Basil Blackwell.

References to *AWL*, *BB*, *LA*, *LFM*, *LPE*, *LWM*, *M*, *NB*, *PG*, and *PR*
are by page number; *LW*, *OC*, *RPPI*, *RPPII*, *RFM*, *ROC*, *TLP*, and *Z*
by section number; *PI* Part I by section number and Part II by page
number.

NOTES

I INTRODUCTION

1 *RPPI* 949–50; *Z* 458
2 *RPPI* 413; *M* 323; *PI* 90–2, 126; *RPPI* 22; *PI* 109
3 *PG* 60
4 *PI* 496
5 *PG* 70
6 *RPPII* 62
7 *BB* 5–6
8 *PI* 122; cf. Rees, R. (ed.) (1987) *Remarks on Frazer's Golden Bough*, Doncaster: Brynmill Press 8–9; *RPPI* 895; *Z* 464. On the translation of 'übersehen' and its derivatives see the translator's note to *PR* 353 and *PG* 491–2.
9 *PR* 1, 39
10 *PI* 130; *RPPI* 633
11 *RPPI* 1054
12 *RPPII* 311; *Z* 465
13 *RPPI* 548
14 *PI* 109, 132; *RPPI* 950
15 *RPPI* 556; *Z* 121
16 *RPPI* 994
17 *RPPI* 257, 723
18 *RPPI* 554; *RPPII* 218, 220–1
19 *RPPII* 730
20 *RPPII* 20, 194; *Z* 112–3
21 *RPPI* 554–8
22 *PI* p. 577, 188; *RPPI* 830; cf. *Z* 49
23 *RPPII* 734
24 *PI* 577
25 *PI* p. 188; *LW* 18

168

26 *RPPI* 45–9, 643; *PI* p. 230; *LW* 209
27 *PI* 182
28 *BB* 26–7; *AWL* 164
29 *RPPI* 212
30 *PI* p. 413, 231, 347; *RPPI* 299
31 *PI* 314. The mistake in the idea that a concept can be elucidated by means of introspection is not the same as the mistake in the idea that a concept can be given sense by 'private ostensive definition'. On private ostensive definition, see Chapter I *Psychological concepts, privacy and behaviour.* and Chapter III *Public and private languages* and *Critique of the private object: II*
32 *RPPI* 836; *RPPII* 64, 148. cf. *Z* 472, 488–92
33 *Z* 466
34 *PI* 371
35 For some elaboration of Wittgenstein's denial that there is a sensation of position or movement, see Chapter VII *Awareness of bodily position and movement* and *The feeling of motion and position.*
36 *Z* 472; *RPPII* 63
37 *RPPII* 45. Wittgenstein also sometimes operated with a concept of a *mental* state which requires a mental state to possess genuine duration. See *Z* 78; *PI* Insert (a) p. 59.
38 *RPPI* 836; *RPPII* 66, 144; *Z* 624. Emotions are not classified as *undergoings* in the first scheme, but are credited with genuine duration in the second scheme. The explanation seems to be that undergoings are defined as not being 'characters of thought', whereas emotions 'colour thoughts'. For an elucidation of the idea of an emotional colouring of thought, see Chapter VII *The emotional colouring of thoughts.*
39 *RPPI* 836
40 *RPPII* 63; *Z* 472
41 *RPPII* 57; *Z* 72
42 *RPPII* 51; *Z* 82
43 *RPPII* 45; *Z* 85
44 *RPPII* 50; *Z* 81
45 *PI* Insert (a) p. 59; *PG* 48; *Z* 71
46 *RPPI* 972–3; *Z* 75–7
47 *Z* 81. The expression 'Marginal note' has disappeared from the square brackets in the second edition of *Zettel*. The marginal note is an afterthought to *RPPII* 50.
48 (1) – (8) fail to apply to intention in the sense of what someone meant by the words he uttered (*RPPII* 274); but an intention in that sense is not an enduring state of any kind.
49 *PI* 281
50 *Z* 471; *RPPI* 286–92; *PI* pp. 179–80; LW 351; *RPPII* 35, 133
51 *RPPII* 75
52 *PI* 571

53 *Z* 471
54 *RFM* III 76; cf. *LFM* 111–12
55 *PI* 321–2

II CONSCIOUSNESS AND THE UNDERSTANDING OF LANGUAGE

1 *PI* 43
2 There is a further difficulty for the intrinsic conception. It requires not only a state of consciousness that contains the rules of chess (for example), but one from which it follows that the subject has decided to play chess, rather than that he has decided not to play chess, or is merely thinking about the game of chess, and so on.
3 *PG* 155; cf. *PI* 196
4 For example: *Z* 44, 45, *PI* p. 217
5 *PI* 149
6 *PI* 572–3
7 See *BB* 3–6
8 See also *BB* 117–8
9 *PI* 156
10 *PI* 157. Cf. *BB* 120–1
11 'Cause and Effect: Intuitive Awareness', *Philosophia*, 6, 1976.
12 *Z* 608; *RPPI* 903
13 *Z* 610; *RPPI* 905
14 *Z* 611; *RPPI* 906
15 *PI* 187; cf. *LFM* 28. Compare also *PI* 684 and the surroundings. Here Wittgenstein makes the point that to say that by my utterance 'It'll stop soon' I meant the pain and not the piano is to say, for example, that I should have given the answer 'pain' then, if I had been asked which I meant.
16 *BB* 142
17 *Z* 16. Wittgenstein's view that the capacity to understand and mean something by a word does not need to be realised in the physical state of the body is not required for this conclusion. For even if this view were false, it would not be the intrinsic nature of any physical state of a person's body that determines what at that time he means.
18 *BB* 5
19 *PG* 47
20 *BB* 65
21 *PI* 28–34
22 *PI* 201
23 *PI* 201. Compare : 'Whenever we interpret a symbol in one way or another, the interpretation is a new symbol added to the old one'. *BB* 33

24 *PG* 47. Cf. *Z* 229. See also *PI* 87
25 *PI* 198
26 *PI* 201
27 Wittgenstein shows as little concern to make this more precise as he does to capture the precise meaning of the sentence 'I meant you to write 1002 after 1000'.
28 'Understanding is like knowing how to go on, and so it is an ability'. *RPPI* 875
29 '"If you had asked me, *this* is the answer I'd have given you." That signifies a state; but not an "accompaniment" of my words'. *RPPI* 675
30 *PI* 199
31 *PI* 199
32 *PI* 202
33 See Peacocke, C. 'Rule-Following: The Nature of Wittgenstein's Arguments', in Holtzman S. H. and Leich, C. M. (eds) (1981) *Wittgenstein: to Follow a Rule*, London: Routledge & Kegan Paul. The interpretation of Wittgenstein's thought put forward by Kripke, S. (1982) *Wittgenstein on Rules and Private Language: An Elementary Exposition*, Oxford: Basil Blackwell, whilst importantly different, also suffers from a failure to represent properly the significance of *PI* 202.
34 Peacocke, C. op.cit., 93–4
35 See, for example, the case of the 'game of chess' in *PI* 200 and 205. See also the passage in *RFM VI*, 34 that follows on from the one quoted in the text.
36 *PI* 199
37 *RFM III* 66–7, *VI* 21, *V* 34, *VI* 43. Compare the question that Wittgenstein raises about voluntary movement: 'If only *one* person had, *once*, made a bodily movement – could the question exist, whether it was voluntary or involuntary?'. *RPPI* 897
38 Wittgenstein's claim that there could not be just one instance of rule-following is explored by Ginet, C., 'Wittgenstein's Claim that there Could not be Just One Occasion of Obeying a Rule', *Acta Philosophica Fennica*, vol.XXVIII, 1976, and McGinn, C. (1984) *Wittgenstein on Meaning*, Oxford: Basil Blackwell, 125 ff.
39 *PG* 145; *Z* 231; *PI* 140, 220
40 *PI* 1
41 Compare *Z* 295: 'the idea that every step should be justified by a something – a sort of pattern – in our mind'.
42 *BB* 143; cf. *PI* 211, 217, 326. The inclination to postulate a strange process that occurs when, for example, I understand how to develop a series in accordance with a rule, is motivated by the reluctance to admit that the chain of reasons has an end.
43 *RFM VI* 35, 38

44 *PI* 228
45 *PI* 207, 237; *RFM VI* 45
46 *RFM VI* 39. Compare *PI* 240–2

III SENSATIONS AND SENSE-IMPRESSIONS

1 Although the qualification in parenthesis appears to be needed, I shall not examine how the distinction between simple and complex properties of sensuous experiences might most plausibly be drawn. I follow Wittgenstein in using the term 'sensation' to cover both sensations and sense-impressions.
2 *RPPI* 720; *ROC* III 313–6
3 *LPE* 320
4 *BB* 47
5 *RPPI* 692
6 *RPPI* 720, 733, 896
7 *LPE passim*, and especially 279, 316; *RPPI* 109, 440, 694.
8 Some inadequacies of the picture are emphasised in my 'Wittgenstein on Sensuous Experiences', *The Philosophical Quarterly*, 1986, vol. 36, 174–95.
9 *LPE* 285
10 Compare *PI* 293: 'how can I generalize the *one* case so irresponsibly?'.
11 *PI* 290
12 *PI* 246
13 *RPPII* 63; *Z* 472
14 *PI* 289
15 *LPE* 319; *RPPII* 63; *Z* 472
16 *PI* 304, 293; *RPPI* 1081–9; *BB* 47
17 *LPE* 319. I have omitted consideration of Wittgenstein's controversial remark 'It can't be said of me at all (except perhaps as a joke) that I *know* I am in pain'. *PI* 246; cf. *LPE* 309. His disinclination to use the word 'know' where doubt is logically excluded is parallel to his reluctance to call the verbal expression of a sensation a *statement* or *report*. See *PI* p. 221; *LW* 881–3; *BB* 30; *RPPI* 775; *OC* 58, 504; *Z* 549; *RPPII* 286–7
18 *PI* 239; *RFM* VII 40
19 *PI* 288, 246, 408; cf. *AWL* 18–9, *M* 307. Likewise this is not a significant proposition: 'I know what "red" means; what I don't know is whether *this* sense-impression is an impression of the colour red'.
20 *PI* 288
21 To assert that the reason I cannot be in error or in doubt about my being in pain is that I am *immediately aware* of the fact is to provide no explanation at all. To say that I am immediately aware of some state of affairs is merely to indicate the *end* of the chain of reasons.

Hence, the picture of a world of consciousness would not be made more adequate by the substitution of the idea of immediate awareness for the idea of an inner sense: a private object of immediate awareness is no more acceptable as a model for a sensation than is a private object of internal observation.

22 'The description of the experience doesn't describe an object. . . The impression – one would like to say – is not an object. . . One can't look at the impression, that is why it is not an object. (Grammatically.)' *RPPI* 1081–9

23 *PI* 374

24 *BB* 14–15, 72–3

25 *PI* 388

26 *PI* 377

27 *PI* 380

28 *LPE* 319

29 *ibid*

30 *PI* 265

31 Compare Kenny, A.J.P. (1973) *Wittgenstein*, London: Allen Lane The Penguin Press, 192–3.

32 *PI* 242; cf. *RFM* VI 39. See Chapter II *Agreement in judgements*.

33 *PI* 244, 256, 288; *RPPI* 313; *LPE* 295.

34 The notion of behaviour, as Wittgenstein uses it, often includes the idea of the external circumstances in which the behaviour (in the narrow sense) occurs. See *RPPI* 314, II 148ff. The vagueness of the idea that words for sensations are 'tied up with' behaviour could not be completely removed, I believe, without attention to the role of the notion of causation in our understanding of such words. I consider this in the final section of the chapter.

35 *LPE* 285–6, 296.

36 *PI* 256

37 *PI* 270

38 *PI* 202

39 See Chapter II *The community interpretation*.

40 *PI* 258

41 *PI* 258, 268

42 *PI* 28

43 ' "To give a sensation a name" means nothing unless I know already in what sort of game this name is to be used.' *LPE* 291. In general: 'if naming something is to be more than just uttering a sound while pointing to something, there must also be, in some form or other, the knowledge of how in the particular case the sound or scratch is to be used'. *BB* 173

44 *PI* 29, 257

45 *LPE* 291

46 *PI* 288

47 *PI* 580

48 *PI* 288

49 *PI* 261

50 *PI* 202

51 *PI* 293

52 *ibid.* In the rest of the chapter I use the simpler expression 'object and name'.

53 *PG* 194; cf. *Z* 248

54 *RPPI* 397

55 *PI* 271

56 *RPPI* 985; cf. *PI* p. 207

57 *BB* 47; cf. 64, 70. Wittgenstein does not elaborate this hint in *The Blue Book.*

58 *PI* 307

59 *PI* 304

60 *BB* 36

61 *BB* 7. Compare: 'the fact that two sentences express the same thought does not mean that there is a thing which is the thought, a gaseous being corresponding to the sentences. But we must not thereupon conclude that the word "thought" as contrasted with "sentence" does not mean anything. The two words have different uses. . .'. *AWL* 55

62 *PI* 304

63 *BB* 73

64 It is clear that when Wittgenstein wrote *Philosophical Grammar* he embraced the view that a pain causes its natural expressions: 'There isn't a further process hidden behind, which is the real understanding, accompanying and causing these manifestations in the way that toothache causes one to groan, hold one's cheek, pull faces, etc.' *PG* 80

65 This is denied by Hacker, P.M.S. (1986) *Insight and Illusion* (revised edition), Oxford: Clarendon Press, 295.

66 Donald Davidson's well-known argument for a general token-token identity between mental and material events is of course based on causal considerations. See his 'Mental Events' reprinted in his *Essays on Actions and Events* (1980) Oxford: Oxford University Press.

67 Wittgenstein's willingness to entertain the possibility that a person's body might lack a nervous system would be inconsistent with his accepting the necessity of a token-token identity of sensations and internal physical events. See *RPPI* 1063; *OC* 4.

68 *PI* 246, 288, 408. I here correct my 'Wittgenstein on Sensuous Experiences', *The Philosophical Quarterly*, 1986, vol.36, 174–95.

69 Witness animals that experience pain but do not self-ascribe pain.

70 *PI* 157; cf. *BB* 120–1. See Chapter II *Dispositions and mental mechanisms.*

71 See Chapter II *Dispositions and mental mechanisms*. Wittgenstein's thesis that a person's verbal expression of thoughts might lie at one end of a chain that terminates inside the person's body in chaos does not allow that the concept of the self-ascription of a sensation requires that a sensation should cause the utterance of the self-ascriptive thought.

IV SEEING ASPECTS

1 These, and many other examples, can be found in numerous places in Wittgenstein's writings. For some of the examples in the text, see *BB* 163–5; many appear in *PI* II xi.
2 *PI* p. 193
3 *RPPI* 1064
4 *LW* 784; *PI* p. 214
5 *RPPII* 242, 245
6 *RPPI* 358
7 *LW* 530
8 Richard Wollheim, 'Seeing-as, seeing-in, and pictorial representation', in his *Art and its Objects* (1980), Second Edition, Cambridge: Cambridge University Press. This notion of seeing one thing in another requires someone who engages in seeing-in to have *two* experiences: an experience of seeing the object in front of the eyes, and an experience of seeing that which is absent. In his book (1987) *Painting as an Art*, London: Thames & Hudson, Chapter II, Wollheim presents a revised, and more plausible, account, which construes seeing-in as a single experience with two aspects, one pertaining to what is present and one to what is absent.
9 Goodman, N. (1969) *Languages of Art*, London: Oxford University Press, especially VI 1. I believe that it is easy to construct counter-examples to Goodman's semiotic theory of pictorial representation, and that an adequate account of pictorial representation must be founded – as Goodman's theory is not – upon a distinctive kind of visual capacity or experience.
10 Peacocke, C. 'Depiction', *The Philosophical Review*, Vol. XCVI, No.3, July 1987.
11 This has been suggested by Kennedy, J. M. (1974) *A Psychology of Picture Perception*, London: Jossey-Bass Publishers, Chapter 6; cf. Peacocke, C. *Sense and Content*, (1983) Oxford: Clarendon Press, 17n.
12 Figure-ground experience is present in other sense-modalities (in the experience of music, for example), where it does not involve pictorial perception, nor perceived relative distance.
13 *LW* 694, 696–7; cf. *PI* p. 207.

14 *RPPI* 1017
15 *RPPI* 970
16 *RPPII* 509
17 *LW* 582
18 *LW* 698, 703; *PI* p. 207; cf. *RPPII* 490, 494, 508
19 *LW* 699
20 *LW* 700, 702; *PI* p. 207; cf. *RPPI* 70, 74
21 *LW* p. 701; *PI* p. 207; *RPPII* 496
22 *LW* 705; *PI* p. 208. What contrast does Wittgenstein have in mind here? When he asserts that the principal aspects of the double cross are not essentially three-dimensional is he claiming that (a) figure-ground experience is not essentially experience *as of* one area (the figure) being in front of the other (the ground), or (b) figure-ground experience is not essentially experience *as if the object were a picture* which represents one area (the figure) as being in front of the other (the ground)? The way in which the possibility of illusion is connected with the three-dimensional aspects of a picture of a three-dimensional thing is this: it is possible to mistake a picture of a three-dimensional object for that object itself (*RPPI* 196; *RPPII* 391, 479).
23 *PI* p. 208; cf. *LW* 530
24 *PI* p. 208
25 Stromberg W. H. (1980) 'Wittgenstein and the Nativism-Empirism Controversy', *Philosophy and Phenomenological Research*, vol.XLI contains a clear and concise account of the Gestalt account of aspect perception and Wittgenstein's criticism of it.
26 Köhler W. (1947) *Gestalt Psychology*, New York: Liveright, Chapter V.
27 *LW* 529–31; cf. *RPPI* 1117
28 *PI* p. 196.
29 *RPPI* 1113 ff.
30 *LW* 444–5
31 *RPPI* 536; cf. *LW* 512
32 On aspects and thought see *Seeing and interpretation* through to *The solution*, this chapter.
33 *PI* p. 196; *LW* 443
34 *LW* 482
35 *LW* 448
36 At *PI* p. 196 Wittgenstein argues that a single consideration is sufficient to undermine the view that the 'organization' of a visual impression is on an equal footing with colour and shape. Compare *LW* 495, 499–503, where the point is presented rather more fully.
37 Peacocke C. (1983) *Sense and Content*, Oxford: Clarendon Press, Chapter 1. I follow the account that Peacocke presents here, although he has since revised, and refined, his conception of the content of experience. See his 'Analogue Content' (The Inaugural

Address, Joint Session of the Aristotelian Society and the Mind Association, London, July 1986). This superior account does not affect the point I wish to make about aspect perception.

38 In *LW* 447 and 451 'Würfelschema' has been mistranslated as 'model of a cube', rather than as 'diagram of a cube' (*LW* 445) or 'schematic cube' (*LW* 499). This assimilates cases that Wittgenstein wished to keep apart.

39 Wittgenstein certainly considered the question whether distance can *really* be seen (*RPPI* 85–86). But the perception and misperception of distance is not an instance of noticing an aspect. The perception of the relative distances of parts of an object *is* the perception of a *property* of the object, in the appropriate sense. See *Aspect perception and interpretation.*

40 *RPPII* 522; *Z* 217
41 *PI* p. 212; *RPPI* 1; *RPPII* 546
42 *RPPI* 8; cf. *PI* p. 212, *RPPII* 547
43 *PI* p. 193; *RPPI* 9
44 *PI* p. 212
45 *LW* 179
46 Ibid
47 *PI* p. 210; *LW* 706
48 *RPPI* 20
49 *PI* pp. 193–4; *RPPI* 3, 9
50 A slight variation of this idea substitutes the thought that A' *occurs whenever* the figure is interpreted in accordance with A for the thought that A' *favours* A. Compare *PI* p. 193 with *RPPI* 9.
51 *RPPI* 13
52 *RPPI* 20
53 *PI* p. 194
54 *RPPII* 360
55 *PI* p. 200
56 The inability to produce the postulated direct description of seeing a figure in accordance with an interpretation, coupled with the conviction that the experience has a nature independent of the interpretation, can tempt us to think: 'I see the figure like *this* (here I point for myself at my visual impression)'. *RPPI* 3
57 *RPPI* 27, 169
58 In some cases of aspect perception it may be necessary for me to focus my eyes, or my attention, on one particular feature or set of features if I am to see the aspect, with the result that some features of the figure are not then noticed. In such a case, there is a sense in which the 'optical picture' does not remain constant through a change of aspect. But Wittgenstein was only concerned with conceptual necessity.
59 Compare the criticism of the notion of the 'organization' of a visual impression.

60 *PI* p. 197; *LW* 544
61 *RPPII* 544
62 *PG* 394; *LW* 612
63 *LW* 451, 488
64 *RPPII* 545
65 *RPPI* 899; *PI* p. 213
66 At least to a certain extent, as Wittgenstein sometimes qualifies the point. *RPPI* 899, 971
67 *RPPI* 899, 976
68 *LW* 452; *PI* p. 213
69 *RPPII* 63, 702; *Z* 477, 627; *RPPI* 899, 976
70 *PI* p. 212; *LW* 516; cf. *LW* 492, 506, 733
71 *RPPI* 1030
72 *RPPI* 316–8
73 *PI* p. 213
74 *RPPI* 8; *PI* p. 212; *RPPII* 547
75 Although there is this similarity, the fact that there is no question of verification or falsification of 'I am seeing this figure as . . .' counts against the view that interpretation constitutes the heart of a change of aspect only if the notion of interpretation is understood in the restrictive fashion Wittgenstein imposes upon it. It does not show that seeing-as is not thinking. For there are ways in which thoughts can be active in the mind in looking at a figure that do not amount to interpreting the figure (in Wittgenstein's sense), and they can be involved in the experience in such a manner that there is no question of verification or falsification.
76 *RPPII* 43
77 *RPPI* 1025; *RPPII* 388
78 *PI* p. 212; *RPPI* 882; *RPPII* 43–5, 51–4, 57, 63. Note the qualification to *RPPII* 50 at *Z* 81. See the discussion in Chapter I *The classification of psychological concepts*.
79 *RPPI* 378, 462. It is for this reason that Wittgenstein insists that 'we must be careful not to think in traditional psychological categories. Such as simply dividing experience into seeing and thinking. . .' (*LW* 542); and that if we try to separate a visual experience from a thought-experience when an aspect dawns, the dawning of the aspect seems to vanish (*LW* 564; cf. *LW* 553–4; *PI* p. 197).
80 *RPPII* 390. Wittgenstein's general anti-reductionist attitude explains his admiration for Bishop Butler's adage 'Everything is what it is and not another thing', which he is reported as describing as 'that marvellous motto' (*LA* III 34).
81 *RPPI* 964; cf. *RPPI* 1038
82 *RPPI* 964, 980–1; *RPPII* 452–3; *PI* p. 200
83 This point should not be confused with the denial that any visual experience must be describable in terms of coloured shapes.

84 *RPPI* 1101–2; *Z* 227
85 *RPPI* 964; cf. *RPPI* 1038
86 *PI* p. 199
87 *LW* 752
88 *LW* 172

V IMAGES, INTERNAL SPEECH AND CALCULATION IN THE HEAD

1 This does not include the category of after-images.
2 For the points in the plan for the treatment of psychological concepts, see *RPPII* 63; *Z* 621. For the other points, see *RPPI* 836; *Z* 623, 627; *RPPII* 65, 85. Many of the points are repeated or elaborated elsewhere.
3 *RPPII* 66, 144; *Z* 624
4 *RPPII* 144
5 *RPPI* 702; *Z* 477
6 *RPPII* 129, 139, 141
7 *RPPII* 86
8 *RPPII* 78
9 Peacocke, C. (1982) 'Wittgenstein and Experience', *The Philosophical Quarterly*, vol.32, no.127.
10 *RPPII* 109, 113–4
11 *RPPII* 79, 90–4
12 *RPPII* 84
13 *RPPII* 83. See also *RPPI* 653
14 *RPPII* 116
15 *RPPII* 88
16 *RPPII* 111
17 *RPPII* 125
18 *RPPI* 885
19 *Z* 632; cf. *RPPII* 88
20 *RPPII* 131
21 This is connected with the point that one cannot follow one's mental images with attention (*Z* 81). Notice that the idea of subjection to the will cannot be applied to aspect perception and imaging in exactly the same sense.
22 Seeing can be both something that happens to me and something I bring about. But when it is, I bring about what happens to me visually *by doing something else*. cf. *RPPII* 91
23 *RPPII* 73, 85, 87; 73, 95, 113–4; 109, 113–4; 112, 124
24 *RPPII* 97
25 *RPPII* 84
26 *RPPII* 96

27 See Roger Brown and Richard J. Herrnstein 'Icons and Images' in Block N. (ed.) (1981) *Imagery*, The MIT Press: Massachusetts.

28 *Z* 635; *RPPII* 100. In *RPPII* 101 Wittgenstein appears to make the point that if my attitude *becomes* observational, then what was a case of imagery becomes a 'fancy'.

29 This is not the same issue as the contentious issue in cognitive science whether the mental representations of imagery represent pictorially or descriptionally. See Block, N. (1983) 'Mental Pictures and Cognitive Science', *The Philosophical Review*, vol.XCII, no.4.

30 It seems clear that Wittgenstein has in mind a particular object, not merely an object of a certain kind.

31 *RPPII* 115

32 Silent speech *to myself* is just one species of silent speech. When I speak silently I no more need speak to myself than when I speak aloud. See *LW* 853

33 *LW* 852; *PI* p. 220

34 For a certain kind of calculating prodigy, see *RPPII* 212–4.

35 *PI* 366

36 *PI* 322

37 *PI* 362

38 Chapter III *Public and private languages* and *Critique of the private object: II*

39 *BB* 7

40 *LW* 854. Wittgenstein points out in *LW* 855 that the relationship between the concepts of tennis and tennis without a ball is not parallel in every important respect to that between the concepts of external and internal calculation or speech and silent speech.

41 *LW* 116

42 *RPPI* 360

43 *RPPI* 657

44 The concept of calculation in the head employs the word 'calculate' in a 'secondary' sense. See *LW* 797–804; *PI* p. 216, 220.

45 *RPPI* 655

46 Compare W's 'auxiliary construction' of the 'Soulless Tribe'. *RPPI* 96–7; *Z* 528–9; *RPPII* 47

47 *PI* 307

48 *RPPI* 652

49 *RPPI* 659

50 *PI* 305, 321

51 *PI* 33–4, 314, 316, 321, 361–3, 369–70; *RPPI* 600

52 *PI* 308

53 *PI* 306

54 *PI* 305

VI THOUGHT AND INTENTION

1 *Z* 122; *RPPII* 215–8
2 *Z* 49; *RPPI* 594, 598, 830
3 *TLP* 3.12, 3.14, 3.5; *NB* 129–30. Cf. Malcolm, N. (1987) *Nothing is Hidden*, Basil Blackwell: Oxford, 64ff.
4 *NB* 82
5 *PG* 152
6 *PI* 329; *PG* 161
7 *PG* 132–62; *PI* 428ff; *Z* 53–70
8 *PG* 134
9 *PG* 140; *PI* 445
10 *PG* 151
11 *PG* 162; *Z* 55
12 *PR* 68
13 *PG* 157; *Z* 68; cf. *PR* 65
14 *PG* 139; *PI* 444
15 *PI* 94
16 *PI* 141
17 *BB* 41
18 'Object of my thought' can mean either 'that which I am thinking' or 'the thing that I am thinking about'. *BB* 38
19 *BB* 36–7; cf. *PG* 146
20 *BB* 37
21 *PI* 139
22 *BB* 37
23 See *Z* 291
24 Cf. Chapter V *Images and pictures*.
25 If I say 'Let's play a game of chess', it is in virtue of my mastery of the English language, my mastery of a technique, that I intend to play chess. See *PI* 197, 199, 337.
26 *PI* p. 217. Cf. *Z* 36: 'One would like to ask: "Would someone who could look into your mind have been able to see that you *meant* to say *that*?"'.
27 *PG* 102
28 See *PI* 572–3
29 *PG* 102
30 Compare the similar point in *Z* 7 about my *writing* to N. Compare also *BB* 38–9, where the connection between word and object in speaking, imaging and thinking is made at another time.
31 *PG* 147
32 *Z* 14, 289
33 *LW* 308. See *LW* 308–18; cf. *RPPI* 262; *PI* p. 177
34 *LW* 96, 277

35 *LW* 107

36 *LW* 817

37 *LW* 827

38 The 'logical germ' is just the 'queer process' of Chapter II, the process that magically contains the use or sense of the expression. Compare: 'To match the words "I grasp the sense" or "I am thinking the thought of this sentence" you hypothesize a process which unlike the bare propositional sign contains these consequences [viz., those embodied in the grammar]'. *PG* 154.

39 *RPPI* 1134–5

40 *PI* 684. See also *PI* 689

41 *RFM* 129

42 *PG* 150

43 *PG* 152

44 *PI* 441. Wittgenstein was happy to concede other uses of 'wish', 'expect', and so on, for which this account would not be appropriate.

45 *Z* 53. If there is no such person as Jack, the content of my expectation (or of any thought supposedly about Jack) is rendered problematic.

46 *PI* 647

47 For some rudimentary points, see *PI* 650, p. 174; *RPPII* 6, 186–8, 224

48 *RPPII* 7

49 *PI* p. 217

50 *PI* 318

51 *RPPII* 7, 257, 266

52 *PI* p. 217

53 *RPPII* 34; *Z* 16

54 *PI* 692–3

VII FEELINGS, EMOTIONS AND THE BODY

1 *RPPI* 351, 803

2 Two compact presentations of Wittgenstein's thoughts about our awareness of the position and movement of our limbs are *PI* II viii and LWM 48–9.

3 The problem is conceptual, not scientific. The nature of the causal explanation of our possession of the capacity for direct knowledge of our bodily position and movement is not what is in question.

4 *RPPI* 698

5 *RPPI* 772

6 *PI* p. 185

7 *RPPI* 798

8 *PI* 321

9 *RPPI* 208, 758
10 *LWM* 49; *RPPI* 406
11 *PI* p. 186; *RPPI* 382, 386, 391
12 *RPPI* 400ff. Since the question is really one concerning the concept of feeling the position and movement of one's body, Wittgenstein's initial use of introspection at *PI* II viii is not vulnerable to the objection that his findings may be true of him but not of others. See *RPPI* 790ff
13 *RPPI* 400–7, 793–4
14 *PI* p. 185; *LWM* 49; *RPPI* 440, 767, 786; *Z* 498; *OC* 417. The positive counterpart to Wittgenstein's denial of the necessity of a local sign is his suggestion that our reaction of touching or pointing to the place of pain determines the place. *BB* 49–50; *RPPII* 63; *Z* 483
15 *PI* p. 185; *LW* 388
16 *RPPI* 452
17 *RPPII* 63. Cf. *RPPII* 499; *Z* 485. The first three characteristics define Wittgenstein's more inclusive category of sensation.
18 *RPPI* 771; *LWM* 48
19 *RPPI* 783
20 *RPPI* 948; *Z* 478
21 *RPPII* 63
22 *RPPI* 770; 948, *LW* 396; cf. *RPPI* 390, 694–5; *Z* 482
23 *RPPI* 784, 786; *Z* 480–1
24 *PI* 624–5. Cf. *RPPI* 394; *LWM* 48
25 Wittgenstein's plan for the treatment of the concept of emotion is at *RPPII* 148, *Z* 488ff. The emotions are the topic of *PI* II i, ix, and there are many remarks on the emotions sprinkled throughout *RPPI*, *II*.
26 *RPPII* 148; *Z* 492
27 *RPPI* 836; *RPPII* 148
28 *RPPI* 836; *RPPII* 148. Cf. *RPPI* 438–40, 803–4; *RPPII* 325; *Z* 495, 497–8, 510
29 *RPPII* 148
30 *RPPI* 836; *RPPII* 153
31 *RPPI* 836; *RPPII* 148
32 *RPPI* 836; *RPPII* 148
33 *PI* 476
34 *RPPII* 148; *Z* 488–9
35 *RPPII* 148; *Z* 492
36 *LA* 13–15; *LWL* 112
37 *RPPII* 148; *Z* 489. The German word is 'Angst'.
38 Wittgenstein indicates that there are restrictions on the emotions that can properly be attributed to languageless creatures, but he offers little in explanation of the nature of these limits. See *PI* p. 650, 174; *RPPI* 314; *RPPII* 308–10; *Z* 518–20; *LW* 358–9

39 *RPPI* 747, 804, 834–6; *RPPII* 153, 306; *Z* 493–4
40 *Z* 493–4
41 *RPPI* 800; *Z* 507
42 *RPPI* 804; cf. *RPPII* 322
43 *RPPII* 160–1; *Z* 50l
44 Chapter IV *Aspect perception and interpretation,* Chapter V *The subjection of images to the will: negative considerations* and *The subjection of images to the will: the positive account.*
45 James, W. (1950) *The Principles of Psychology,* vol. 2, London: Dover Publications, Chapter XXV.
46 Op cit. 452
47 ibid
48 op.cit. 450–1
49 op.cit. 451
50 *BB* 103
51 *PI* 321
52 *RPPI* 925; *Z* 503
53 op.cit. 450, 462
54 op.cit. 450
55 *LW* 414–5
56 *RPPII* 148; *Z* 492, 496
57 *RPPI* 728, 730; *Z* 499. Compare *RPPI* 924: 'Compare a dreadful fright and a sudden violent pain. It is the sensation of pain that is dreadful – but is it the sensation of fright? When someone falls headlong in my presence, – is that merely the cause of an extremely unpleasant sensation in *me*? And how can this question get answered? Does someone who reports the frightful incident complain of the sensation, the catching of breath, etc.? If one wants to help someone get over the fright, does one treat the body? Doesn't one much more soothe him about the event, the occasion?'
58 *RPPI* 454
59 *RPPII* 157
60 *RPPII* 321.
61 *RPPII* 148, *Z* 488: 'But the sensations are not the emotions. (In the sense in which the numeral 2 is not the number 2.)'
62 Compare his comments on James's view of the 'self' at *PI* 413.
63 *RPPI* 457. Cf. *RPPI* 133, 135; *RPPII* 171, 500; *PI* p. 188
64 *PI* 321. The same point applies to Wittgenstein's rejection of the thesis that any sensations I experience when I attend to the position or movement of my body I will also experience when my attention is otherwise engaged.
65 *RPPII* 321; *LW* 415
66 *Z* 487

INDEX